CB129961

Learning Stars

Maths Book 1

Contents

Unit 1	Hello	2
Unit 2	My school	10
Unit 3	My toys	18
Unit 4	On the farm	28
Unit 5	My body	36
Unit 6	My clothes	44
Unit 7	I like picnics!	54
Unit 8	Run and jump!	62
Unit 9	In the kitchen	70
Unit 10	Let's have a party!	80

MACMILLAN

Jill Leighton

Unit 1
Lesson 1

Hello

1 Trace and colour.

1

Trace Bella and Horsey.
Colour Bella pink and Horsey brown.

2 Find and draw. Say.

2

Find Bella.
Trace the path with your finger from Horsey to Bella.
Draw the path.
Say who you can see: Mum, Dad, Grandma, Grandpa, Lily and Jack.

1 Lesson 2

1 Match.

2 Circle.

1 Match the people and animals to where they live: e.g. Does Bella live in the house or the garden?

2 Find and circle the picture that is different.

3 Trace and colour.

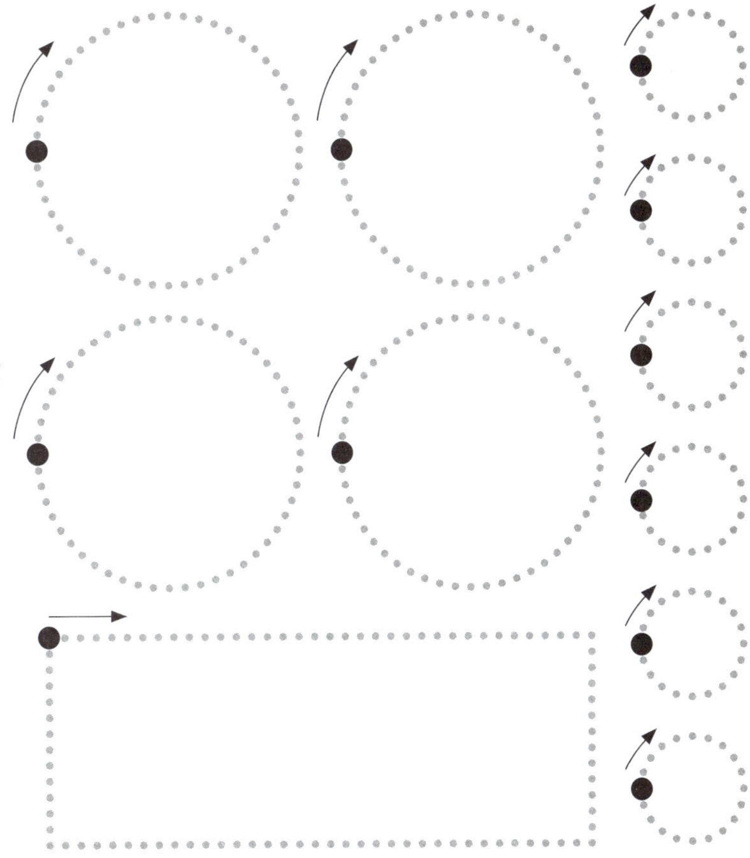

4 Trace and match.

3

Trace and colour the circles red.

4

Trace Bella's circles and match them to the correct silhouettes.

1 Find and circle.

2 Say and draw.

1

Find and circle the four pictures of Horsey and Bella.

2

Say the sequence. Draw the last pictures in the series.

3 Count. Trace and write.

one 1

4 Find 1. Circle.

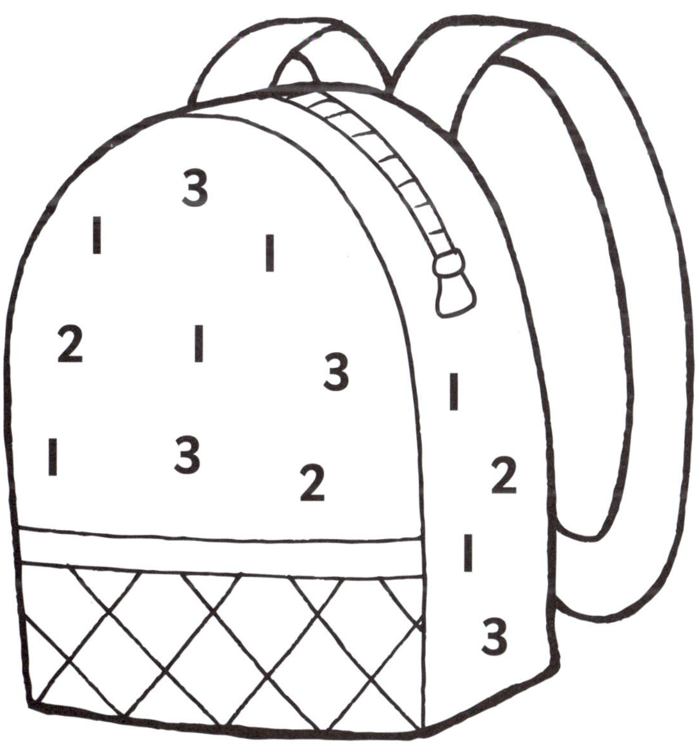

5 Find 1. Colour.

3 Count the book. Trace and write number 1 and the number word one.

4 Find the 6 number ones on the bag and circle them.

5 Colour the tables that have 1 book.

1 Match and say.

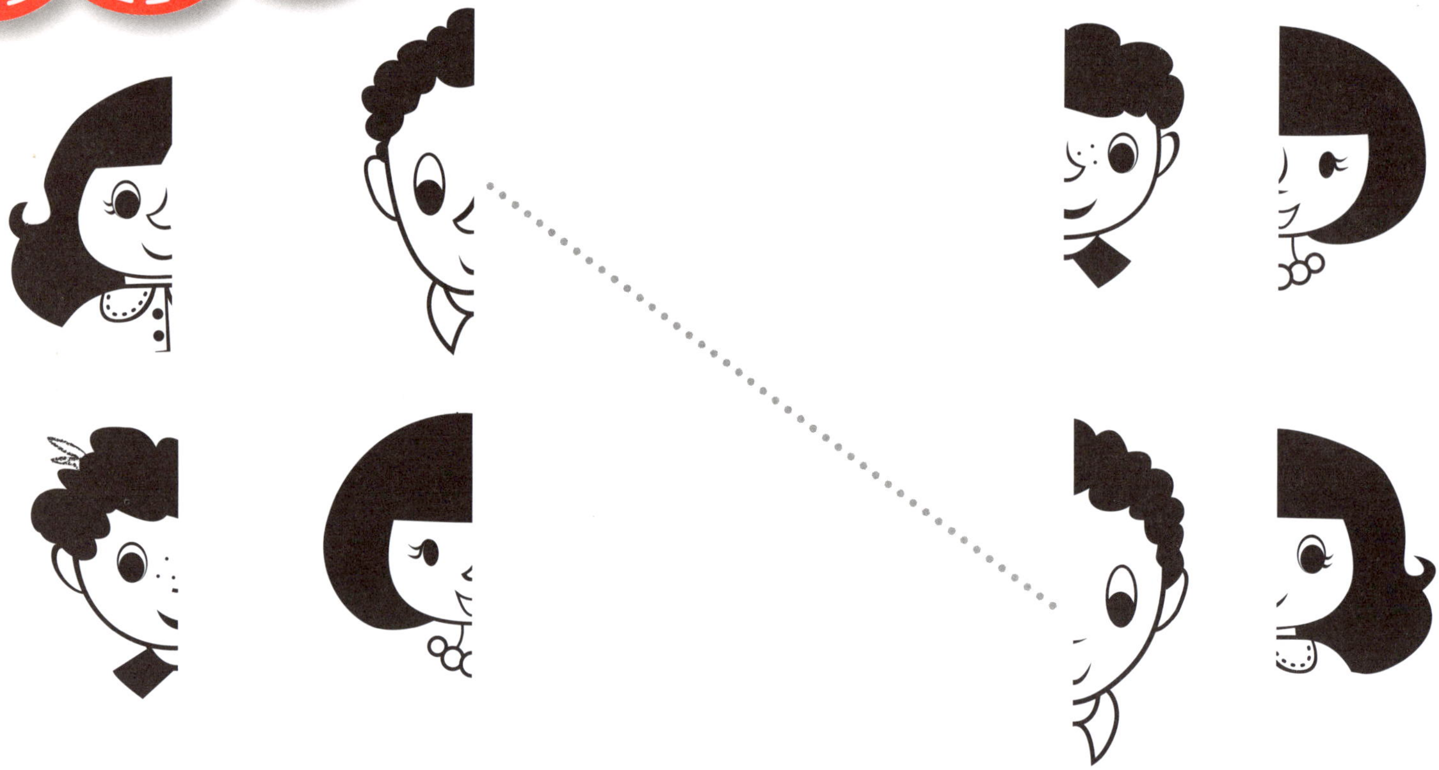

2 Circle.

1 Match the two sides of the face and say the names of the characters.

2 Circle the correct final picture.

3 Count and write.

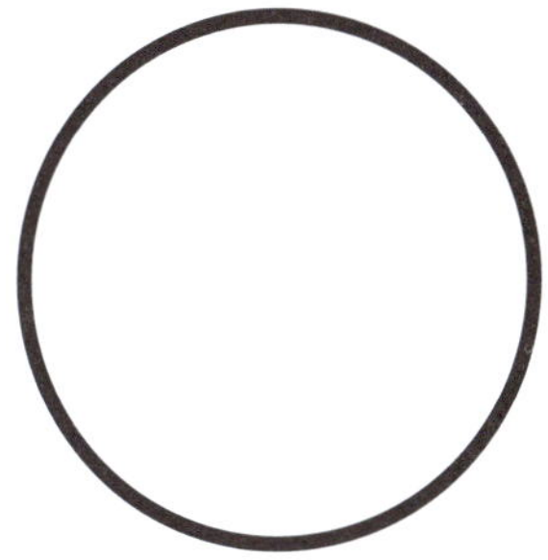

4 Trace. Find 1 and circle.

3 Count the items and write number 1 in each box.

4 Trace number 1 on the number line. Then find and circle 1 ant hidden in the garden.

Unit 2
Lesson 1

My school

1 Count. Trace and write.

2 two

2

2 Trace. Count and write.

2

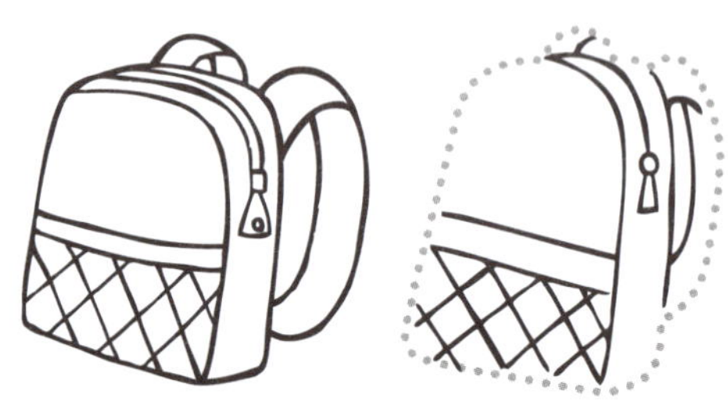

1 Count the crayons. Trace and write number 2 and the number word two.

2 Trace the second picture and count the items. Write the total in the box.

3 Trace, count and write.

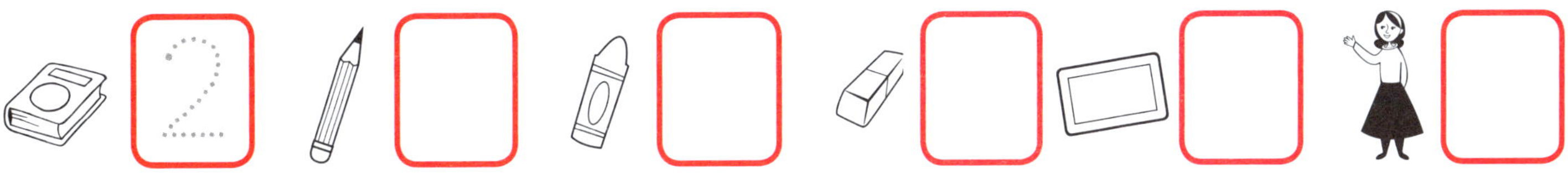

4 Circle.

3

Trace a line from Jack and Lily to the school. Count and write 1 or 2 in the total box.

4

Circle the picture that is different.

1 Trace and match.

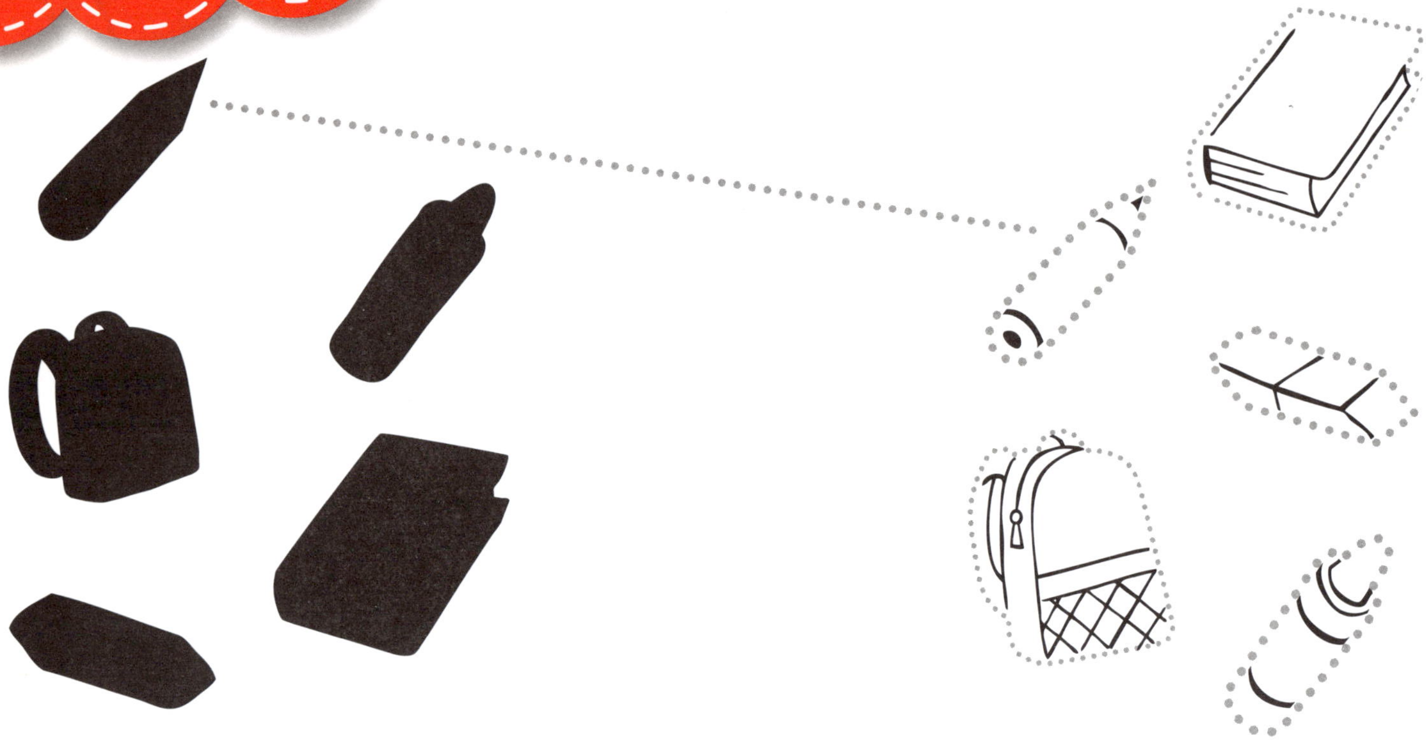

2 Match.

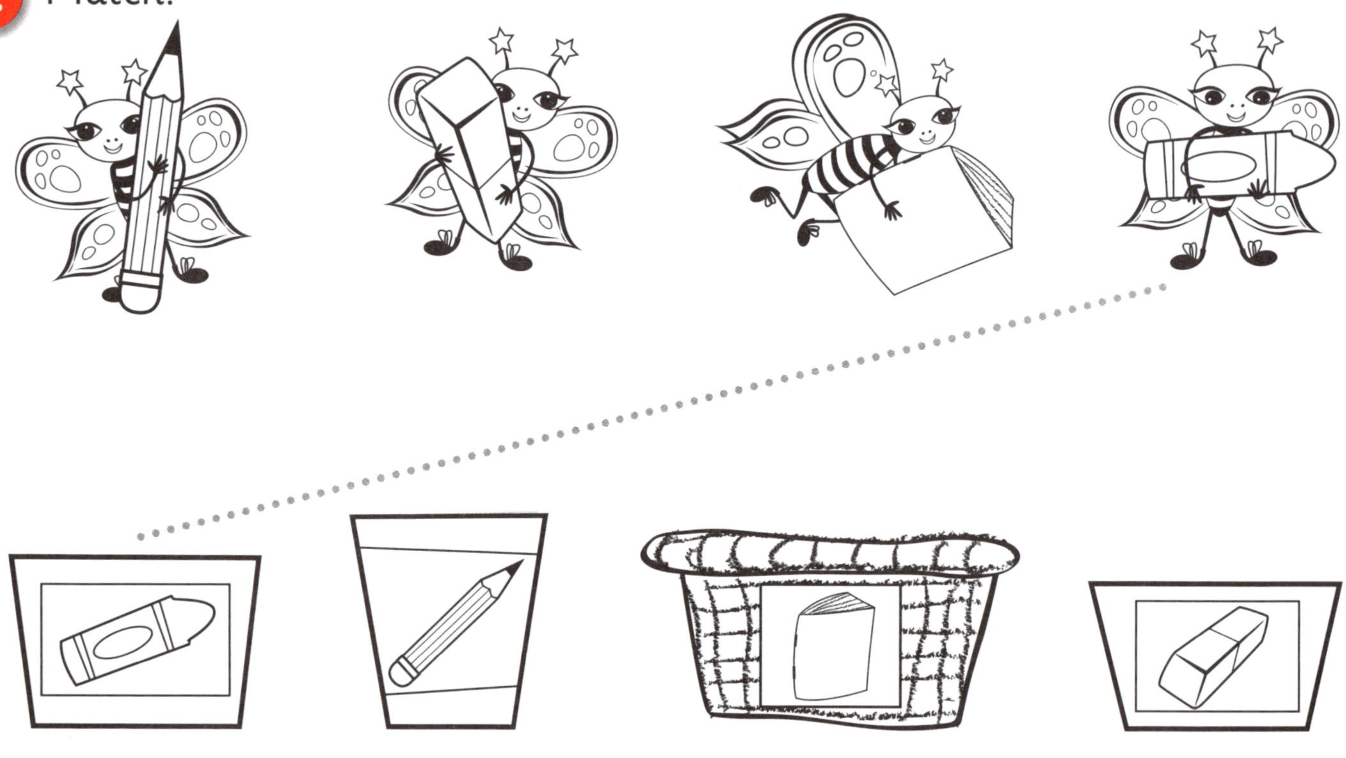

1

Trace the pictures on the right. Match the silhouettes to the same picture.

2

Match the item to the correct container.

3 Complete and colour.

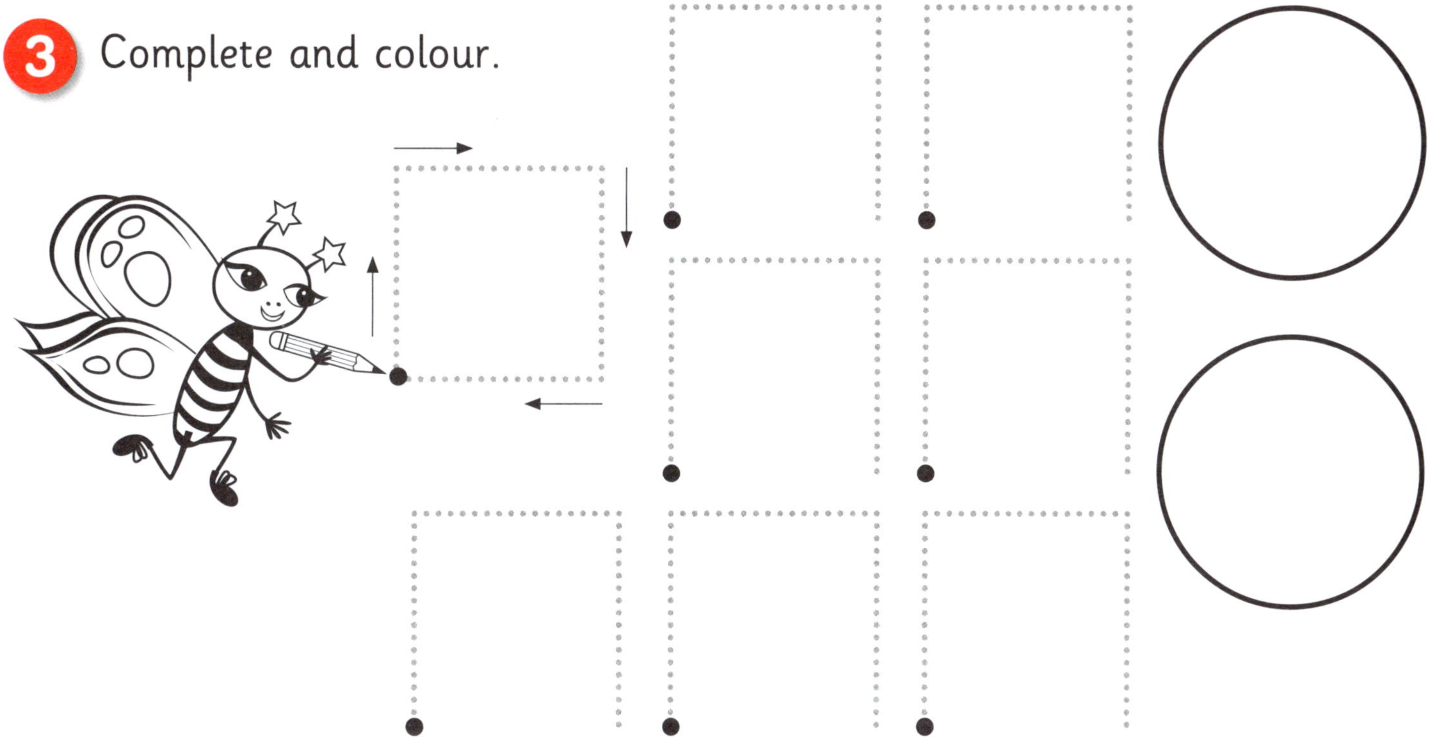

4 Find and circle groups of 2.

3

Finish drawing the squares. Colour the squares green and the circles red.

4

Draw a circle around the groups of 2.

1 Trace, colour and circle.

2 Trace and draw.

1 

Trace the sun, rain and rainbow. Colour the rainbow red, yellow, pink, blue, green, pink, purple and orange. Then find and circle Bella.

2 

Trace the sun and the rain. Finish drawing the rainbow.

3 Draw.

4 Trace and draw.

3 Draw the next picture in the series.

4 Trace the lines on the t-shirts. Draw lines on the last t-shirt.

2 Lesson 4

1 Count and match.

2 Count and write.

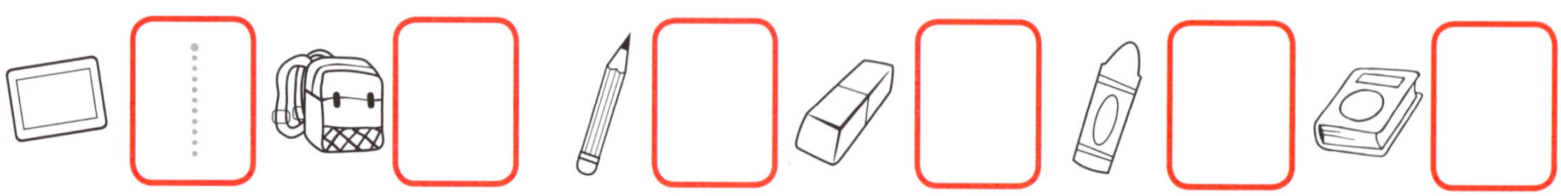

1 Count the items. Match the number to the correct number of items.

2 Count the items and write the totals in the box.

3 Count and write.

4 Trace. Find 2 and circle.

3 Count the school objects. Write 1 or 2 in the box.

4 Trace two balls in the basket. Then find and circle 2 pencils hidden in the garden.

Unit 3
Lesson 1

My toys

1 Count. Trace and write.

3 three

3

2 Trace. Count and write.

3

1 Count the bears. Trace and write number 3 and the number word three.

2 Trace the toy, count and write the total in the box.

3 Count and circle 2.

4 Count and circle 3.

1 2 3 1 2 3 1 2 3 1 2 3 1 2 3

5 Count and match.

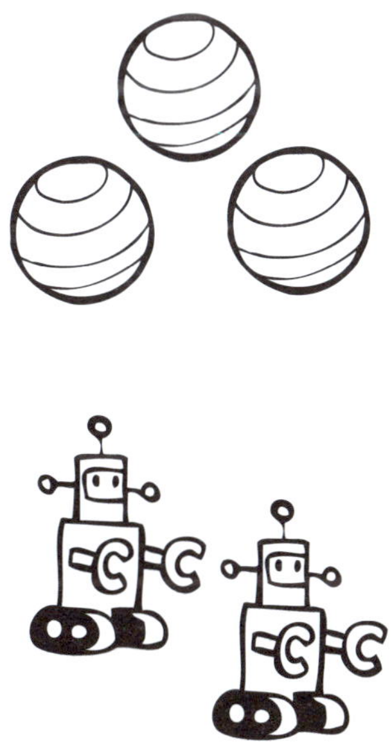

3

3 Count the toys and circle the number.

4 Count the toys and circle the number.

5 Count the toys and match number 3 to groups of 3 toys.

3 Lesson 2

1 Find and circle.

1 Find and circle the picture which is different.

2 Complete and colour.

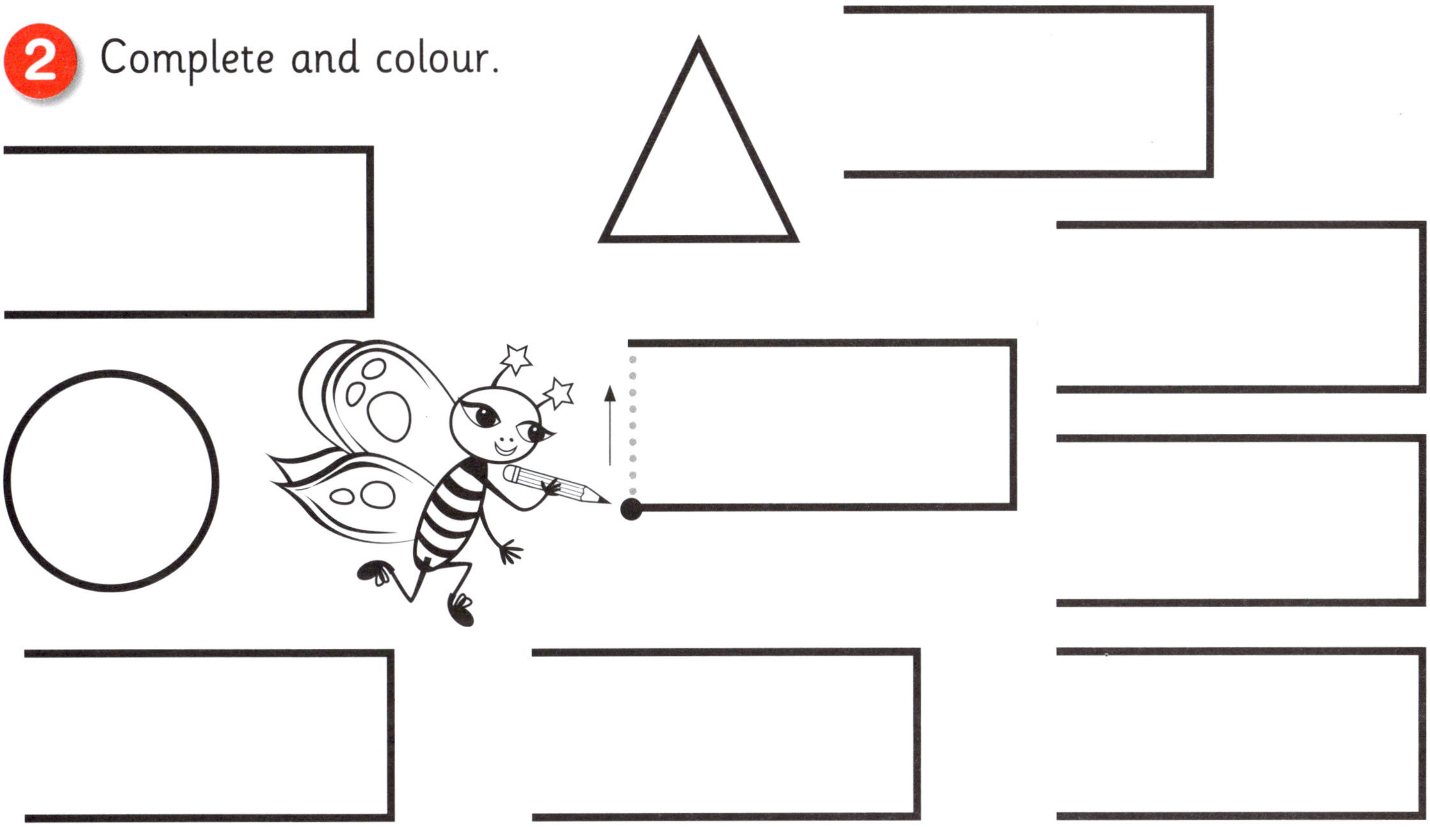

3 Find and colour.

2 Draw 1 line to complete the rectangles. Colour the rectangles yellow, circle red and triangle green.

3 Find 3 rectangles inside each robot and colour.

1 Circle.

2 Match.

1 Draw a circle around the group of big toys and a circle around the group of small toys.

2 Match the small toys to the small toybox and the big toys to the big toy box.

3 Draw.

4 Count and write.

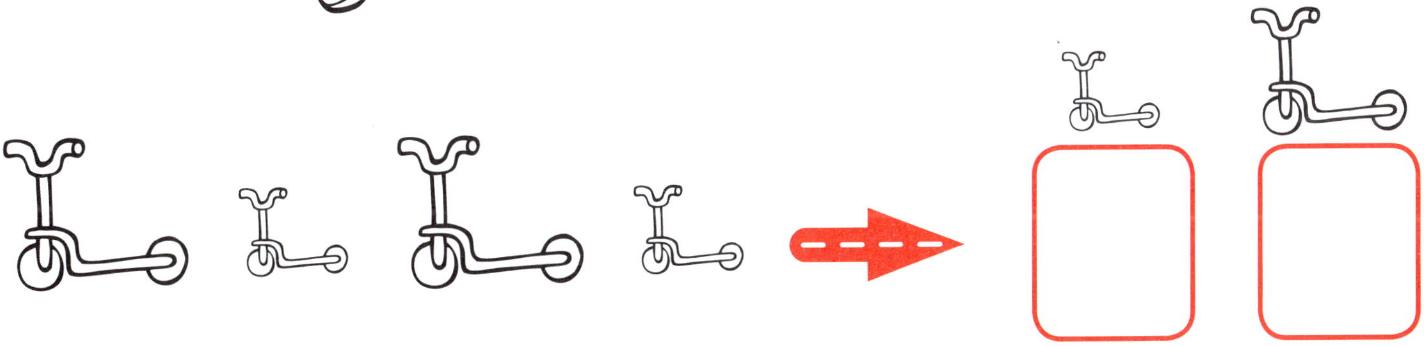

3

Draw the next picture.

4

Count the small toys first and write the total in the box. Then count the big toys and write the total in the box.

3 Lesson 4

1 Count and match.

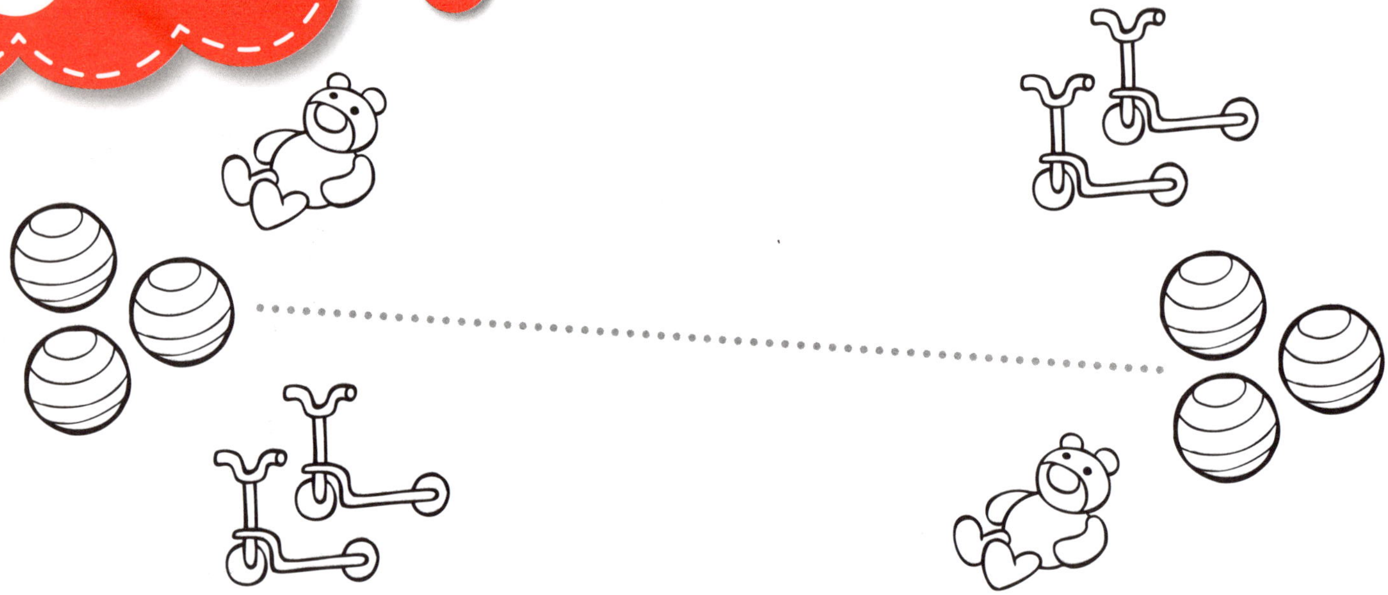

2 Count and circle.

1 2 3

1 2 3

1 2 3

1 2 3

1 2 3

1 2 3

3 Write.

1, 2, 3, 1, 2, 3, ___, ___, ___

1 Count and match groups with the same number.

2 Count and circle the correct number for each group.

3 Write the numbers.

4 Trace. Count and write.

5 Trace. Find 3 and circle.

4 Trace the pictures. Then count and write the total in the box.

5 Trace numbers 1, 2 and 3. Then find and circle 3 bees hiding in the garden.

Review 1

1 Count and colour.

1 

2 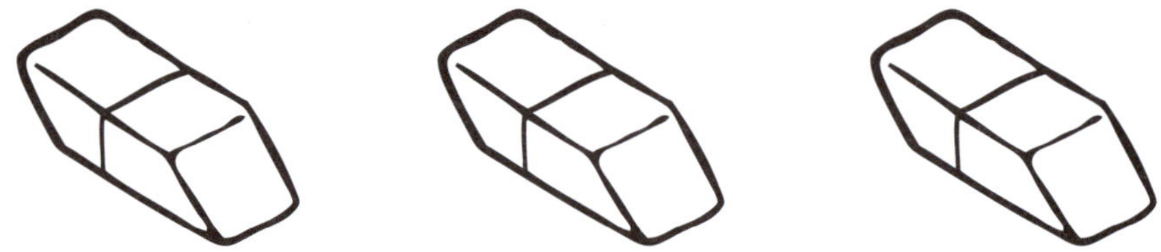

3 

2 Draw.

1 Count and colour the correct number of items.

2 Follow the sequence and draw the next picture.

3 Count and circle.

1 2 3

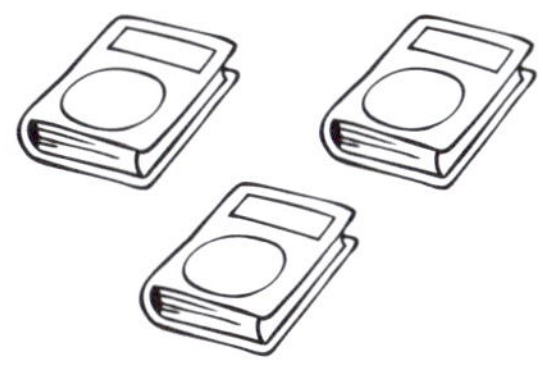

1 2 3

1 2 3

1 2 3

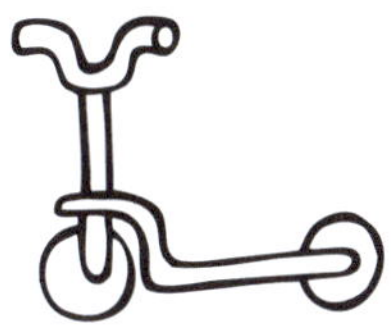

1 2 3

1 2 3

4 Match.

3 1 2

two three one

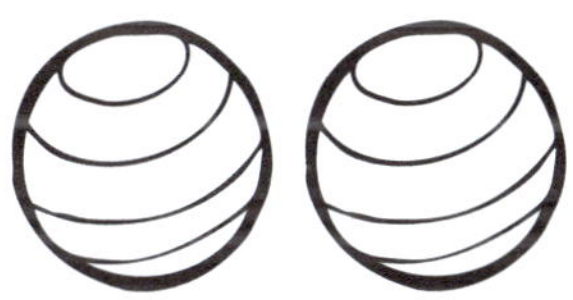

5 Count and write.

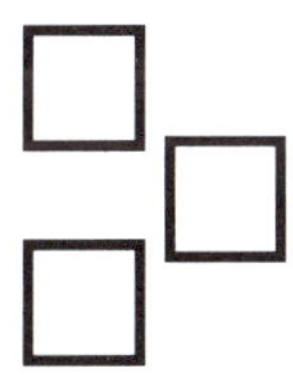

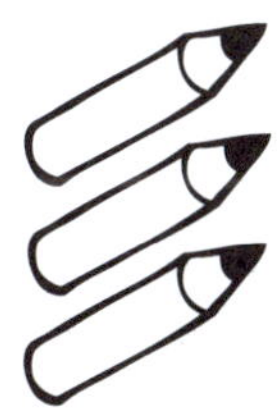

3 Count each group of items and circle the correct number.

4 Match the numbers, number words and groups of items by drawing a line.

5 Count the items and write the total in the box.

Unit 4 Lesson 1

On the farm

1 Count. Trace and write.

4 four

4

2 Find and circle.

1 Count the cats. Trace and write number 4 and the number word four.

2 Find the correct number of animals and circle them in the main picture.

3 Count and colour.

1 2 3 4

1 2 3 4

4 Count and write.

3 Count and colour the correct number.

4 Count the animals and write the totals in the box.

1 Jump 1. Draw and write.

1 2 3 4 | 3

1 2 3 4 |

1 2 3 4 |

2 Find 4. Circle.

1

Jump 1 with Horsey.
Draw a line and write the correct number in the box.

2

Find and circle groups of 4 animals.

3 Complete and colour.

4 Count and write.

3

Draw 1 side and complete the triangles. Then colour the triangles.

4

Count the triangles and circles on the chicken and write the total in the box. Then repeat for the duck.

1 Trace and match.

2 Circle.

1 Trace through the maze to help the baby animals find their mothers.

2 Find the picture that is different and circle.

3 Find, circle and colour.

3

Count the groups of animals on the right side of the page and circle the correct number in the main picture. Then colour the animals.

4 Lesson 4

1 Count and write.

2 Count and write.

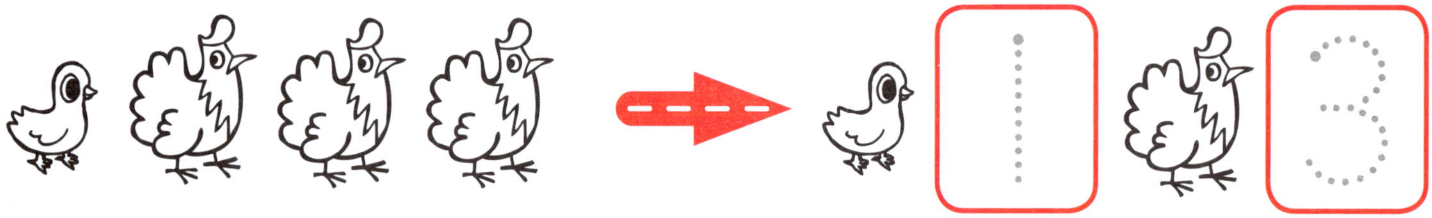

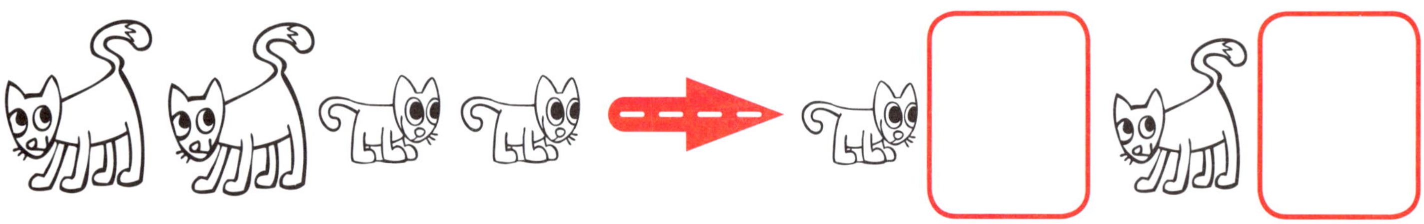

1 Count the groups of animals and write the total in the box.

2 Count and write the number of baby and mummy animals. Write the total in the box.

3 Draw.

4 Trace. Find 4 and circle.

3 Draw the correct numbers of chickens.

4 Trace numbers 1,2,3 and 4. Then find and circle 4 cats hidden in the garden.

Unit 5
Lesson 1

My body

1 Count. Trace and write.

5 five

5

2 Match.

1 Count the fingers. Trace and write number 5 and the number word five.

2 Match Horsey's big ear, eye, nose, mouth and mane to the small ones in the mirror.

3 Draw.

3

Draw the missing body parts in each picture.

1 Count and write.

2 Match and draw.

1 Count the fingers and write the missing numbers.

2 Match the puzzle piece to the correct space in the main picture. Then try to draw the missing piece in the main picture.

3 Draw and colour.

4 Count and write.

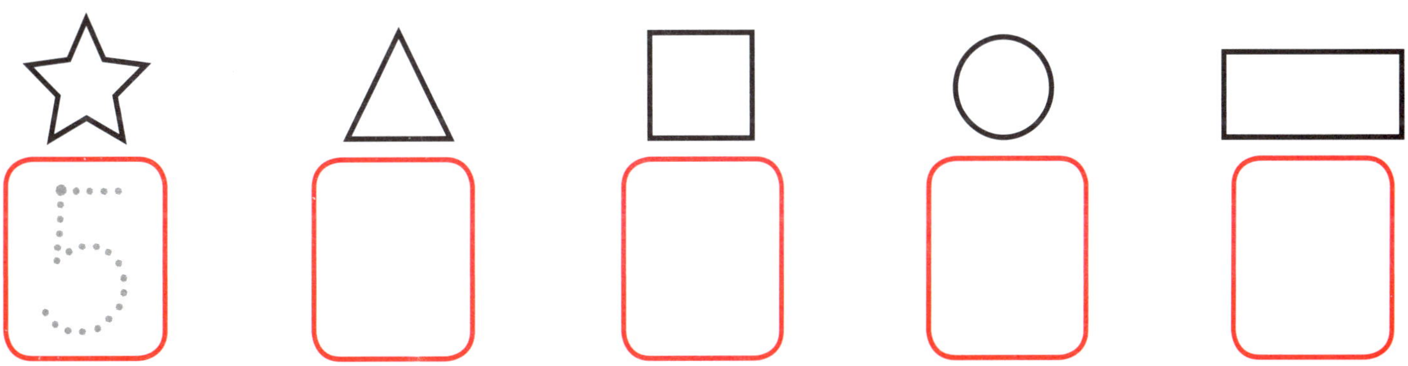

3

Draw and colour the shapes. Then draw your face in the mirror.

4

Count the shapes in activity 3 and write the total in the box.

1 Match.

2 Circle.

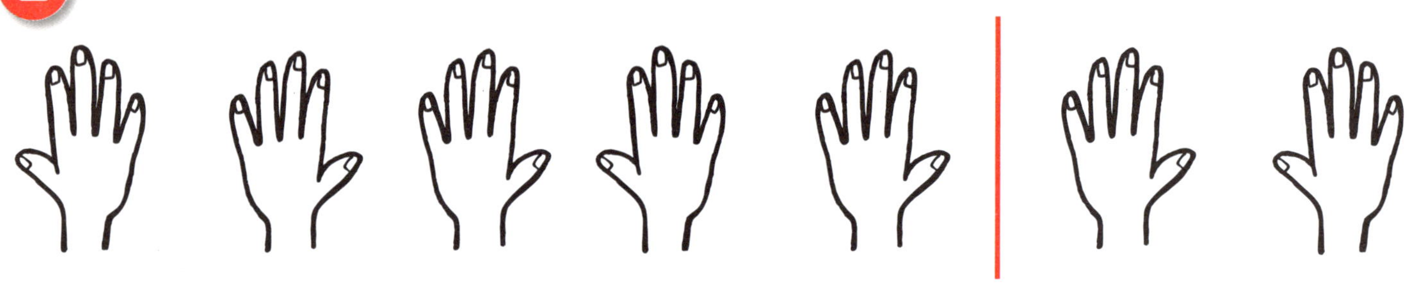

3 Circle or colour.

1 Match the children doing the same action.

2 Circle the next picture.

3 Circle the picture on the right and colour the picture on the left.

4 Find and circle.

4

Find the picture which is different and circle.

1 Jump 1.

1 2 3 4 5 3

1 2 3 4 5

2 Jump 2.

1 2 3 4 5 5

1 2 3 4 5

3 Count and circle 5.

1 Jump 1 and trace a line. Write the number in the box.

2 Jump 2 and trace lines. Write the number in the box.

3 Count and circle the group of 5.

4 Match and draw circles.

1 ········ one ········

2 two

3 three

4 four

5 five

5 Trace. Find 5 and circle.

4 Match and draw circles.

5 Trace numbers 1, 2, 3, 4 and 5. Then find and circle 5 buns hidden in the garden.

Unit 6 Lesson 1 My clothes

1 Count. Trace and write.

6 six

6

2 Count and write.

1

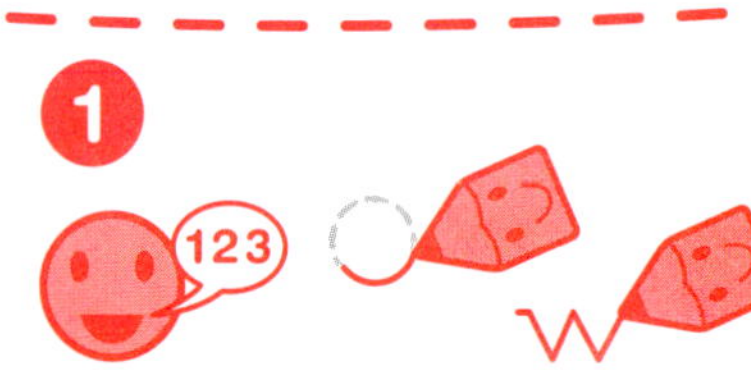

Count the t-shirts. Trace and write number 6 and the number word six.

2

Trace the last item in each group. Then count and write the total in the box.

3 Match and colour.

4 Find and circle.

3

Match. Then colour groups of 5 red and groups of 6 blue.

4

Find and circle the matching item.

1 Circle, count and write.

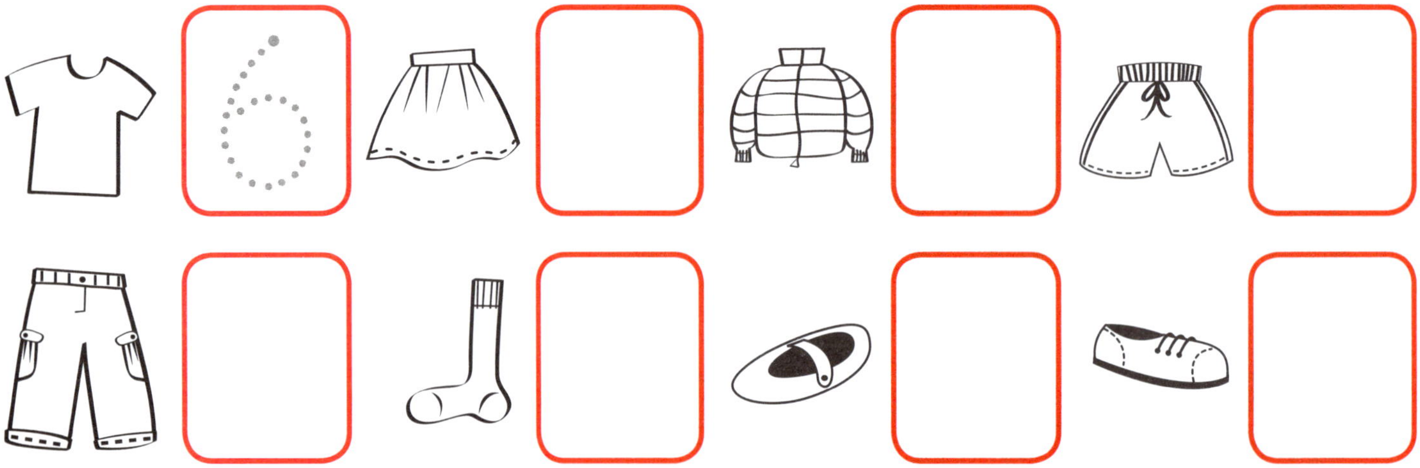

1

Circle each group of clothes. Then count and write the total in the box.
Colour the clothes, e.g., t-shirts blue.

2 Count, write and circle.

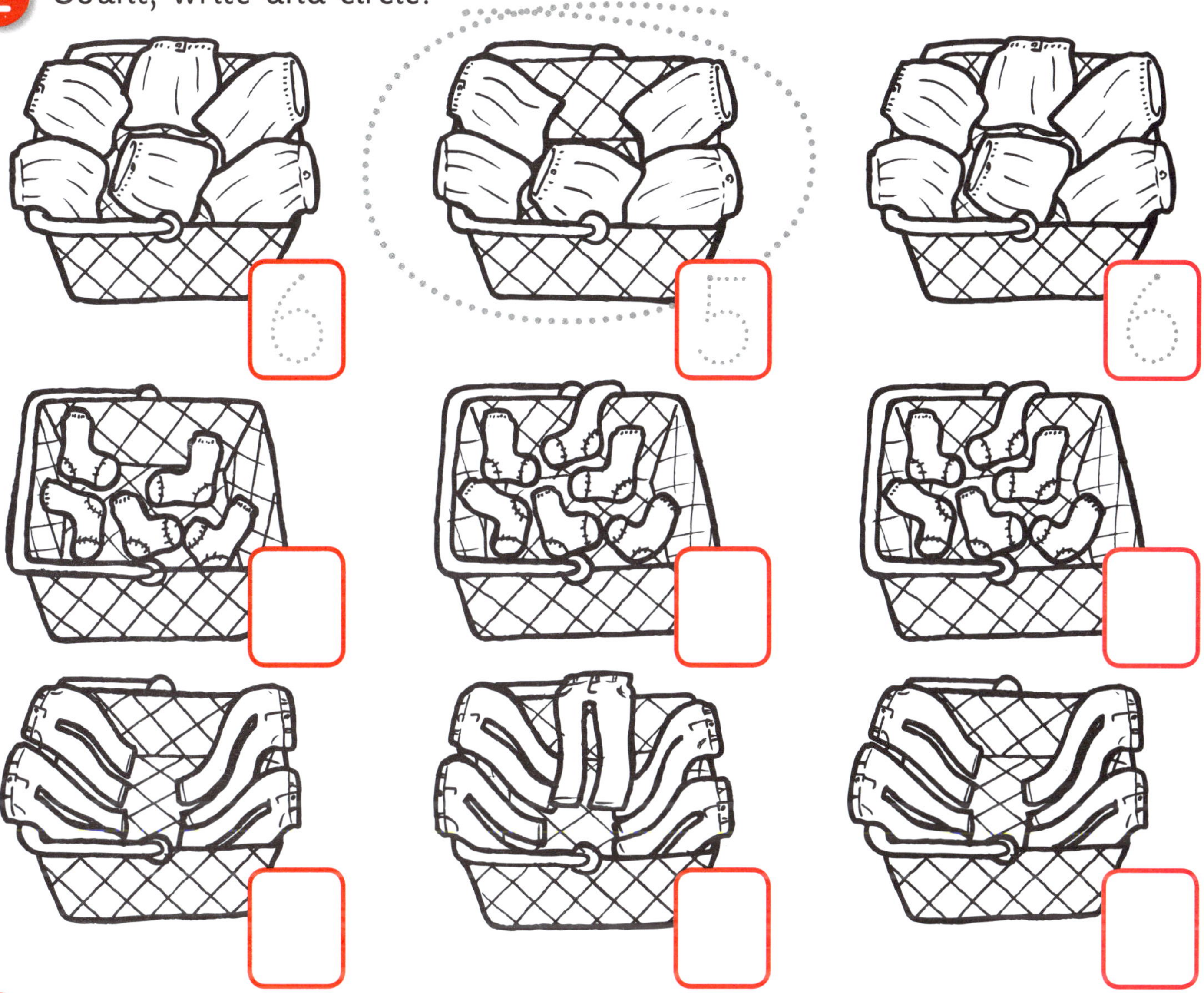

3 Draw and say.

2 Count and write the number. Then circle what is different in each row.

3 Draw the next two pictures. Then say e.g., 'right sock, left sock, right shoe, left shoe'.

1 Match.

4		six
2		four
3		two
1		three
6		one
5		five

2 Draw.

six one six one

five two

four three

three two five four

1 Match the numbers and words to the spots.

2 Read the numbers and draw a line to join them in the correct order to make the shape of a sock.

3 Match.

4 Draw.

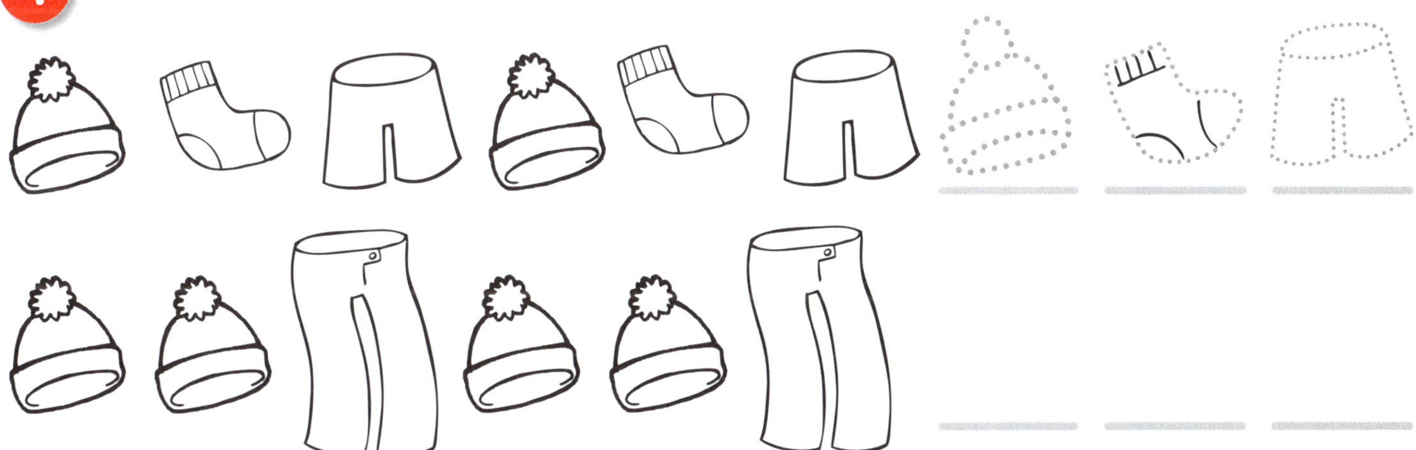

3 Match the clothes to the hot or cold window.

4 Draw the next 3 items in the series.

1 Match.

2 Draw.

1 Match the clothes in the main picture to the patterns.

2 Draw the next pattern in the series.

3 Count and write. Colour.

4 Trace. Find 6 and circle.

3 Count and write. Then colour the biggest group.

4 Trace numbers 1,2,3,4,5 and 6. Then find and circle 6 socks hidden in the garden.

Review 2

1 Count and match.

1

2

3

4

5

6

2 Count and circle.

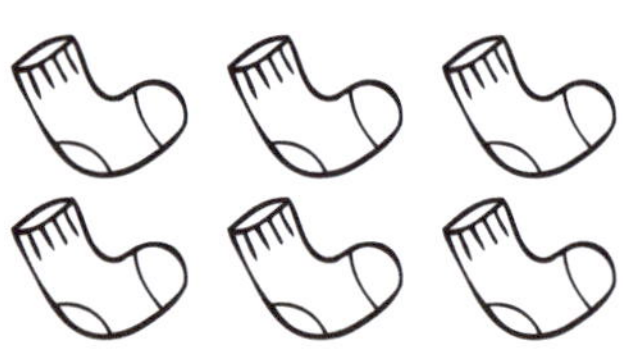

6 4 5

3 2 4

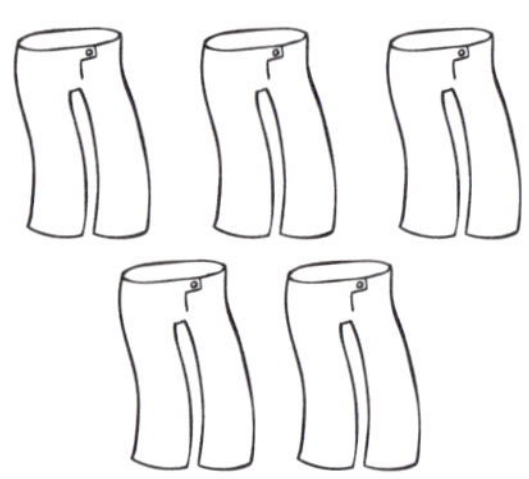

3 4 6

5 4 6

6 4 5

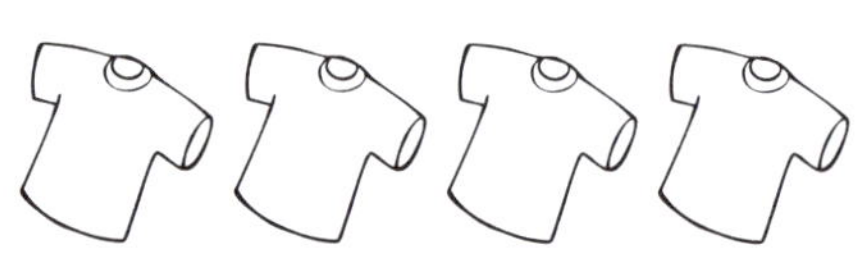

5 6 4

1 Count the groups of animals and match them to the correct number by drawing a line.

2 Count the items in each group and circle the correct number.

3 Count and write.

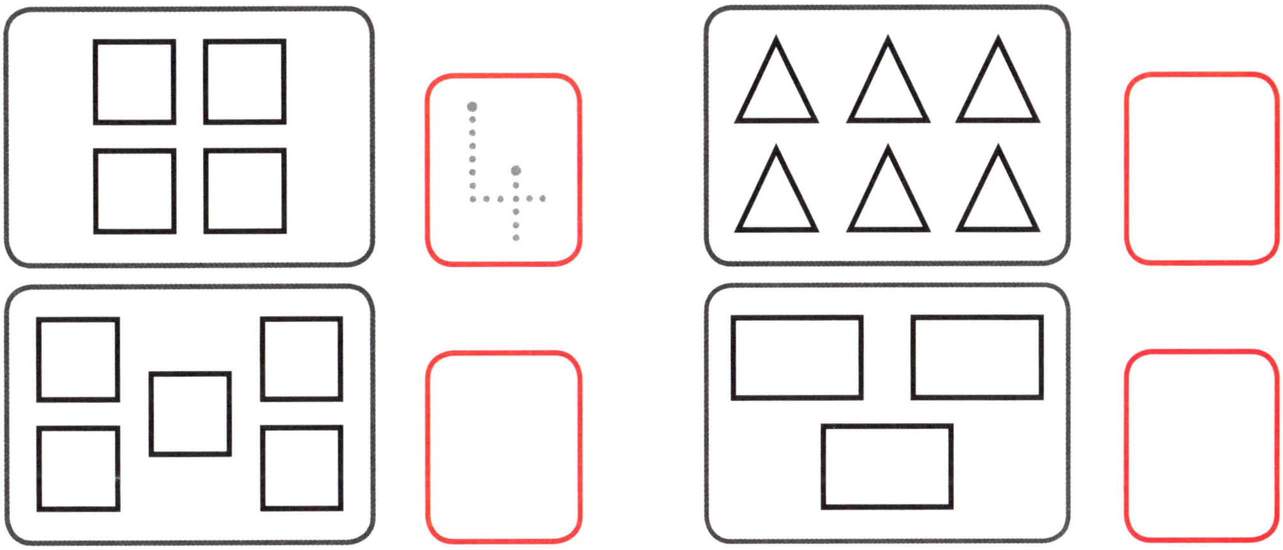

4 Count and write.

5 Circle.

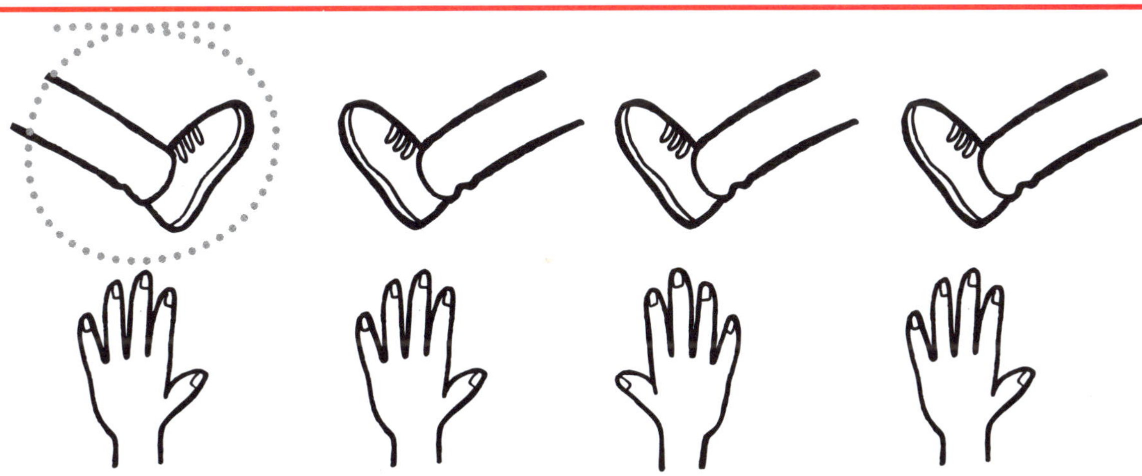

3 Count the shapes and write the total in the box.

4 Count the baby and adult animals. Then write the totals in the boxes.

5 Circle the odd one out.

Unit 7
Lesson 1

I like picnics!

1 Count. Trace and write.

7 seven

7 7 7 7 7 7 7 7

2 Count and circle.

4 2 5

7 5 6

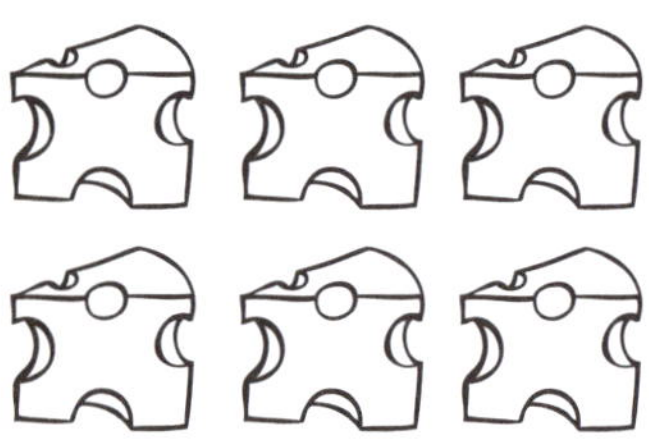

5 6 7

6 5 7

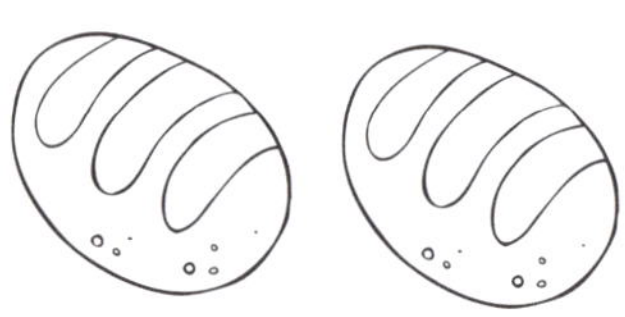

2 3 4

3 6 4

1 Count the apples. Trace and write number 7 and the number word seven.

2 Count the food items and circle the correct number.

3 Match.

4 Count and colour.

colour 6

colour 4

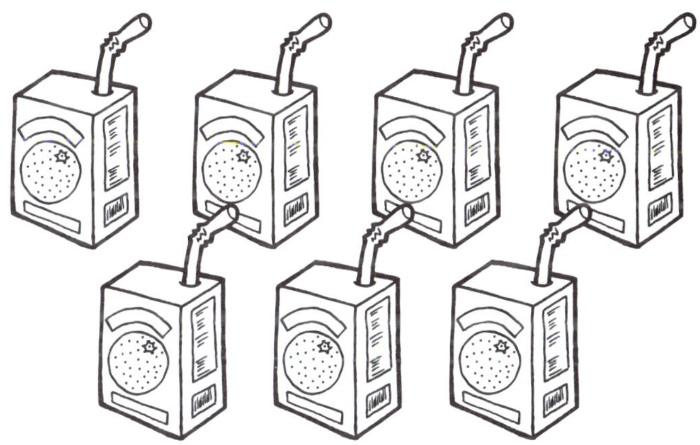

colour 5

colour 7

3 Match the two shopping baskets which are the same.

4 Count and colour the correct numbers of fruit and vegetables in the pictures.

7 Lesson 2

1 Count and match.

2 Draw.

1 Count and match the food to the correct number on the mat. Then draw a line.

2 Say the sequence and draw the last two pictures in the series.

3 Draw.

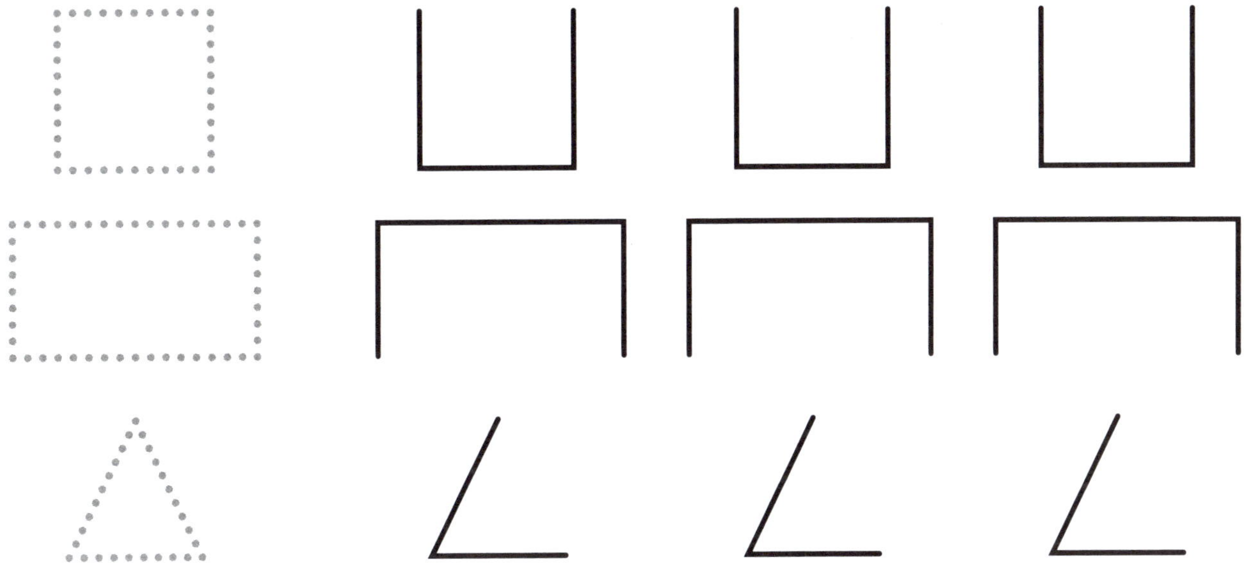

4 Match.

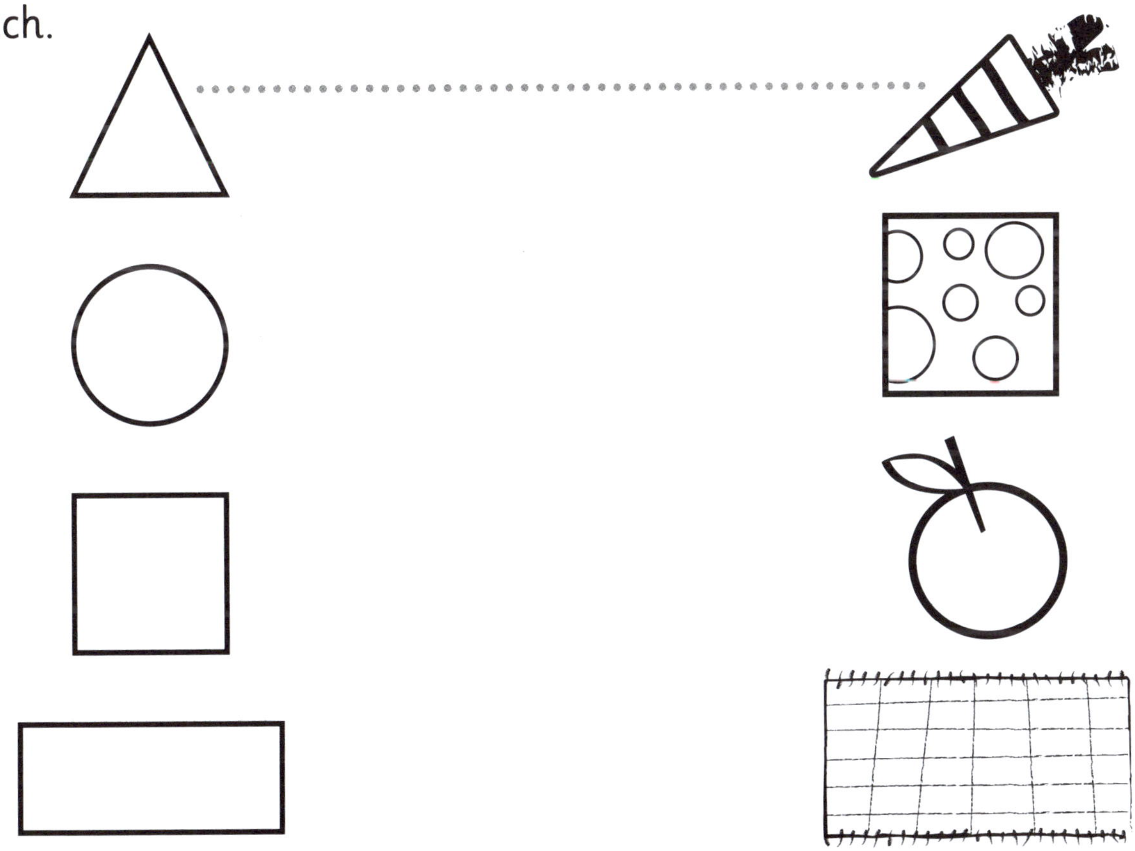

3 Draw the missing lines and complete the shapes.

4 Match the shape to the correct item.

7 Lesson 3

1 Find, count and write.

2 Draw.

1

Find and count the items in the big picture. Write the total in the box.

2

Draw pictures to finish the sets.

3 Count and write.

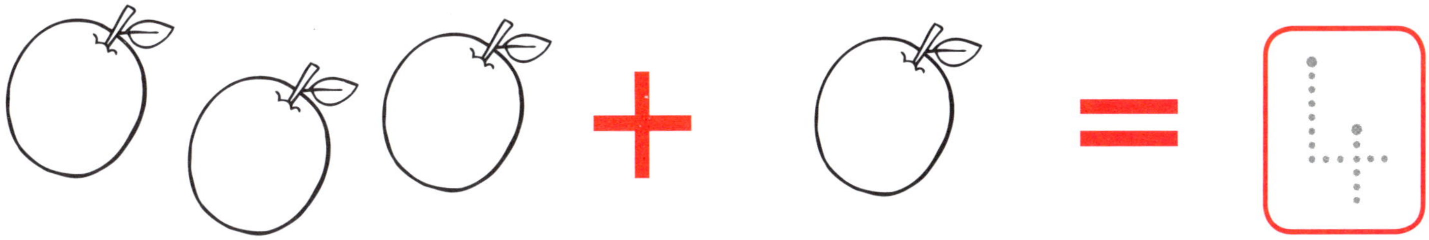

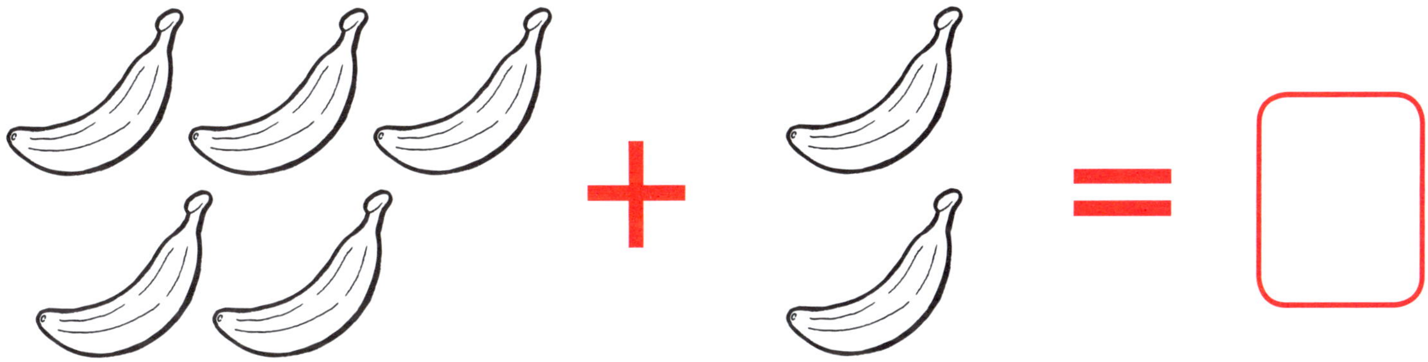

4 Count and write.

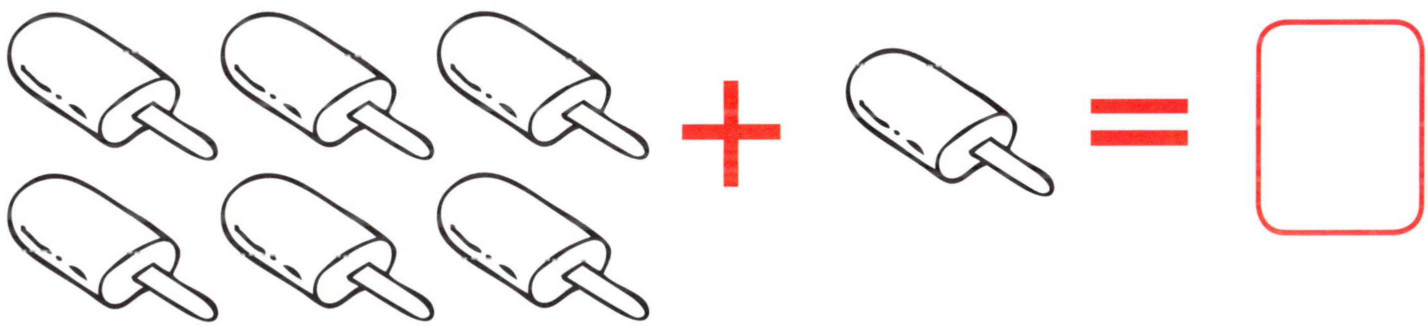

3 Count and write the total.

4 Repeat for the unhealthy foods.

7 Lesson 4

1 Circle 0.

2 Match.

3 Trace.

0 1 2 3 4 5 6 7 8 9 10

1 Circle zero. Circle the plates that are empty.

2 Match the numbers to the correct basket.

3 Trace numbers 0 1 2 3 4 5 6 7 on the number line.

4 Draw.

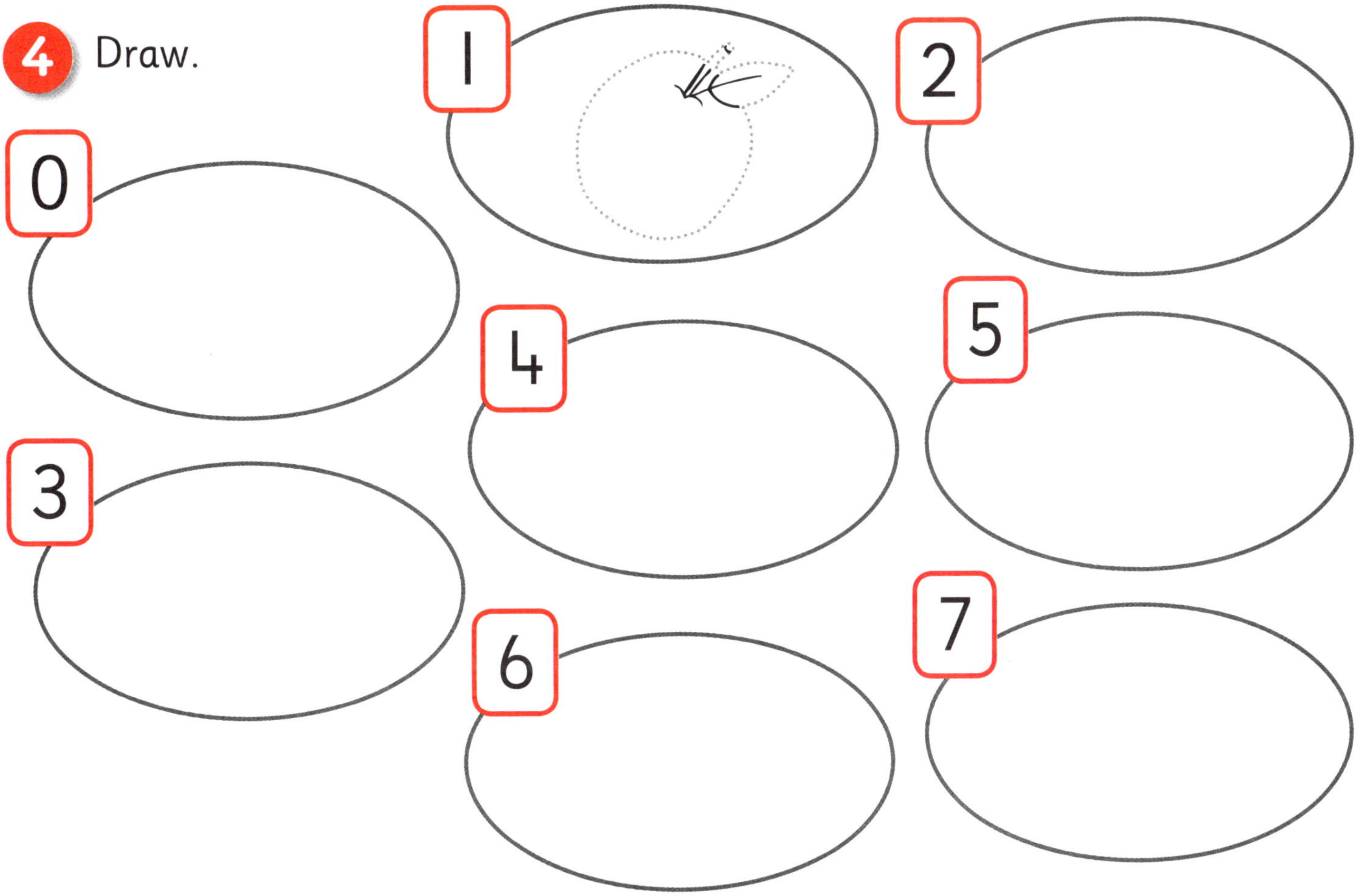

5 Trace. Find 7 and circle.

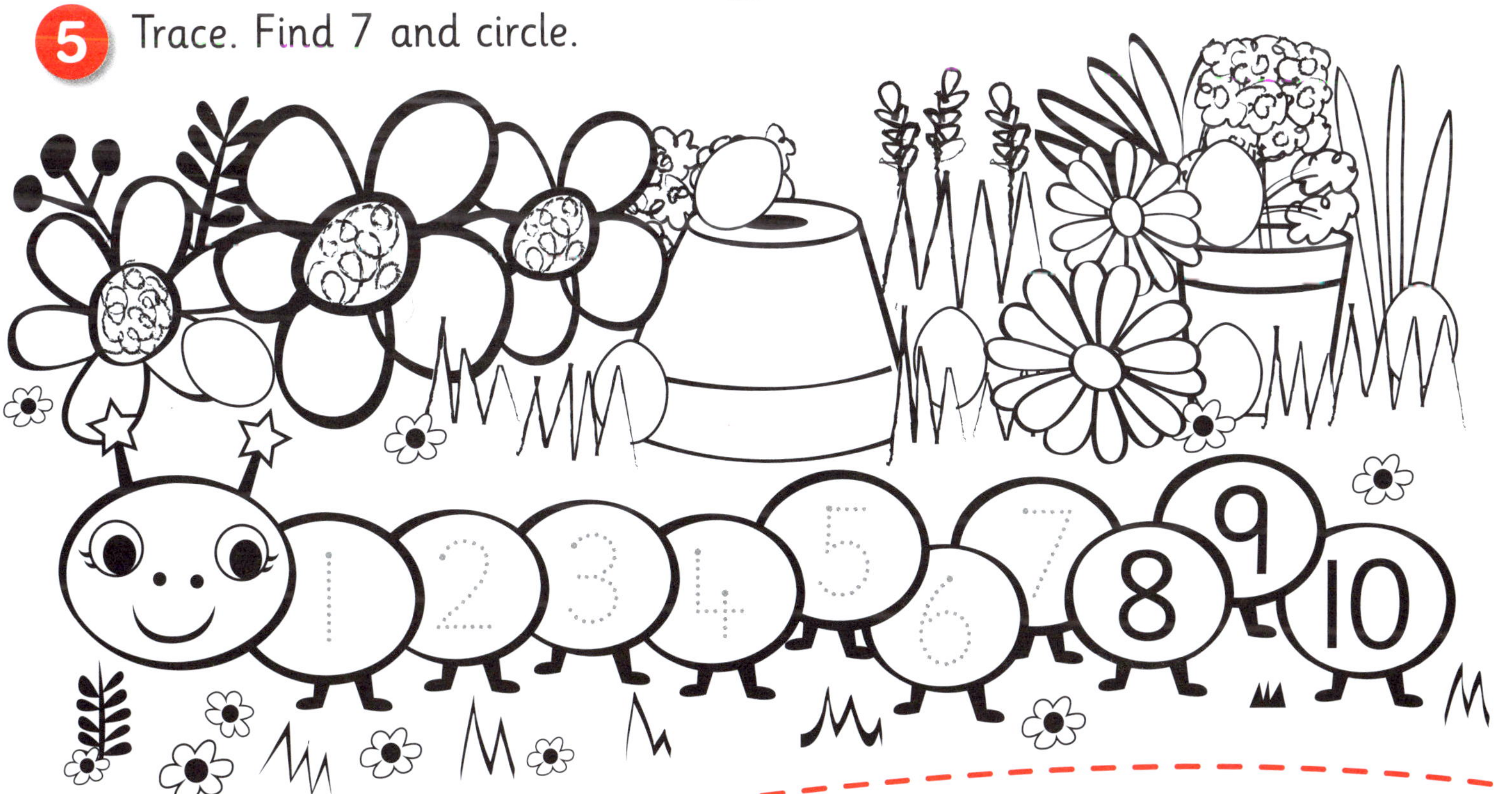

4 Draw the correct number of apples on each plate.

5 Trace numbers 1 2 3 4 5 6 and 7. Then find and circle 7 eggs hidden in the garden.

Unit 8 Lesson 1 Run and jump!

1 Count. Trace and write.

8 eight

8

2 Circle.

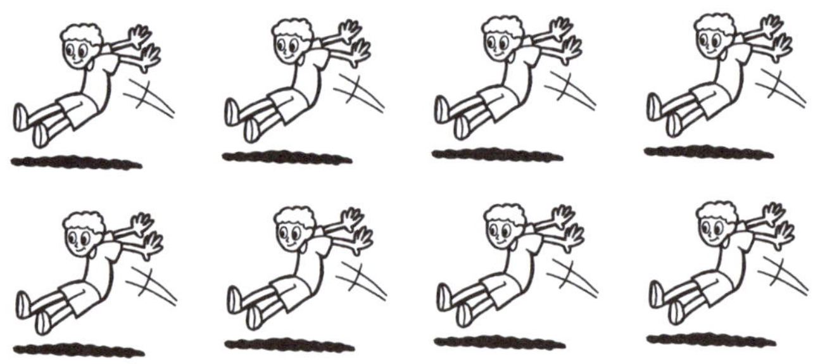

1 
Count the bean bags. Trace and write number 8 and the number word eight.

2 
Count the number of children in each group and circle the bigger group.

3 Colour.

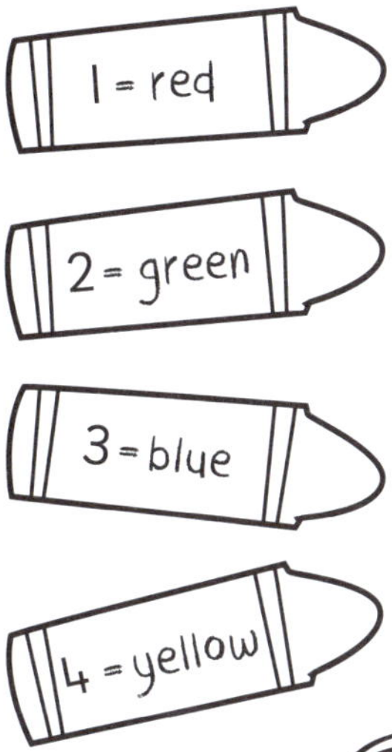

4 Match and colour.

3 Colour the crayons the correct colour. Then colour the bean bags according to the key.

4 Match the bean bags which have the same number and number word together. Then colour the matching pairs the same colour.

1 Write.

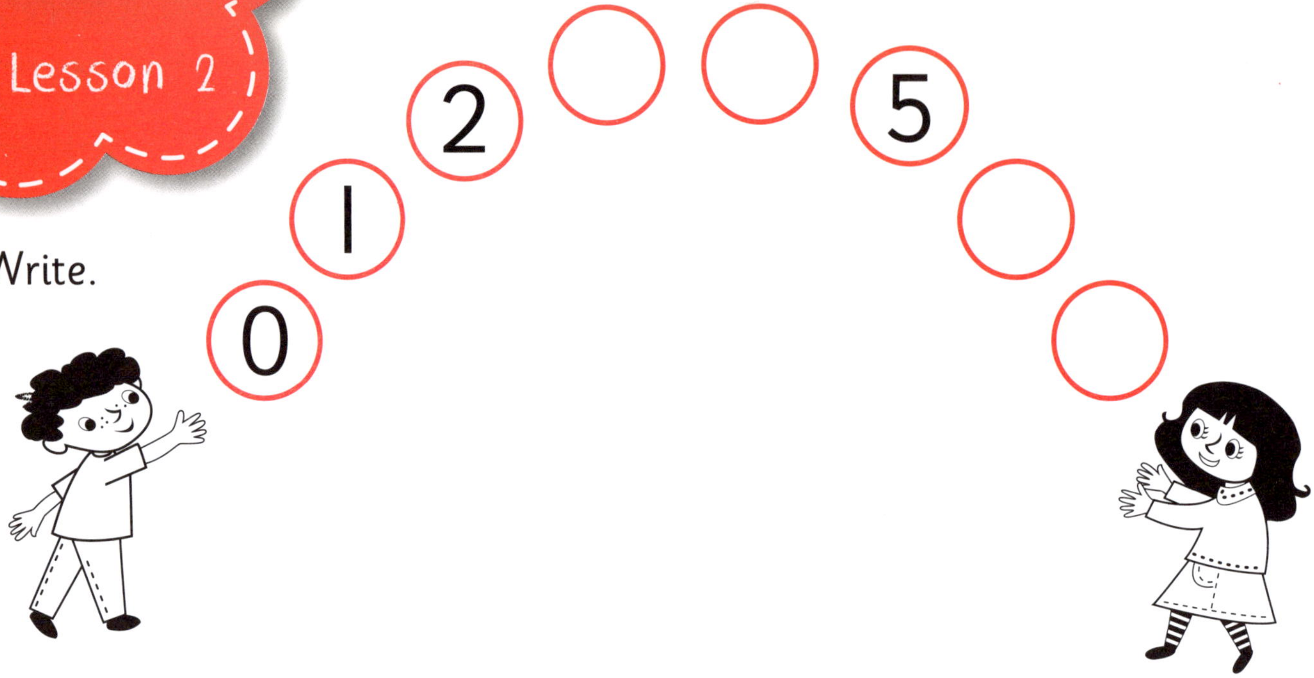

2 Count and circle.

1
2
3
4
5
6
7
8

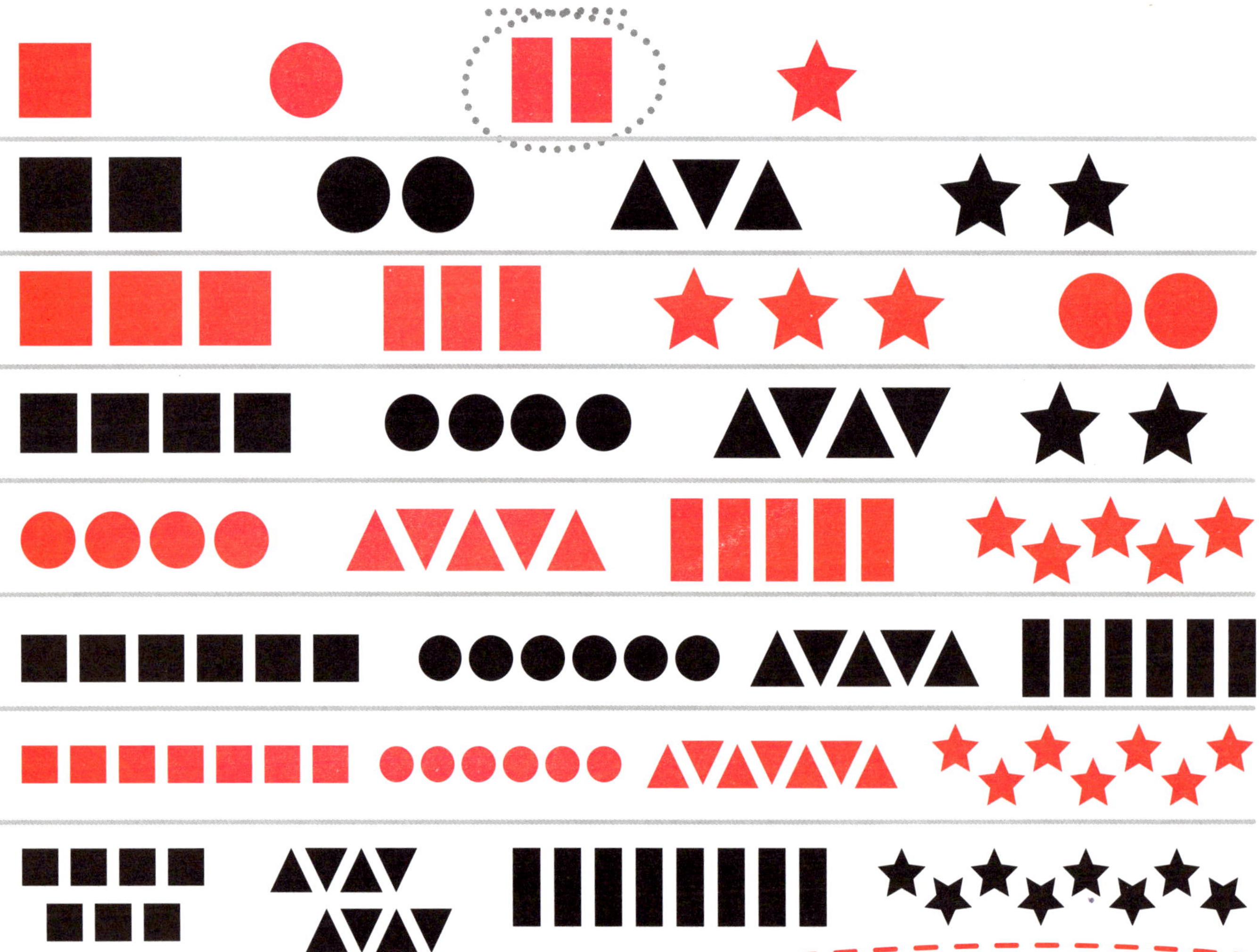

1 Write the missing numbers.

2 Circle the odd one out.

3 Circle, count and write.

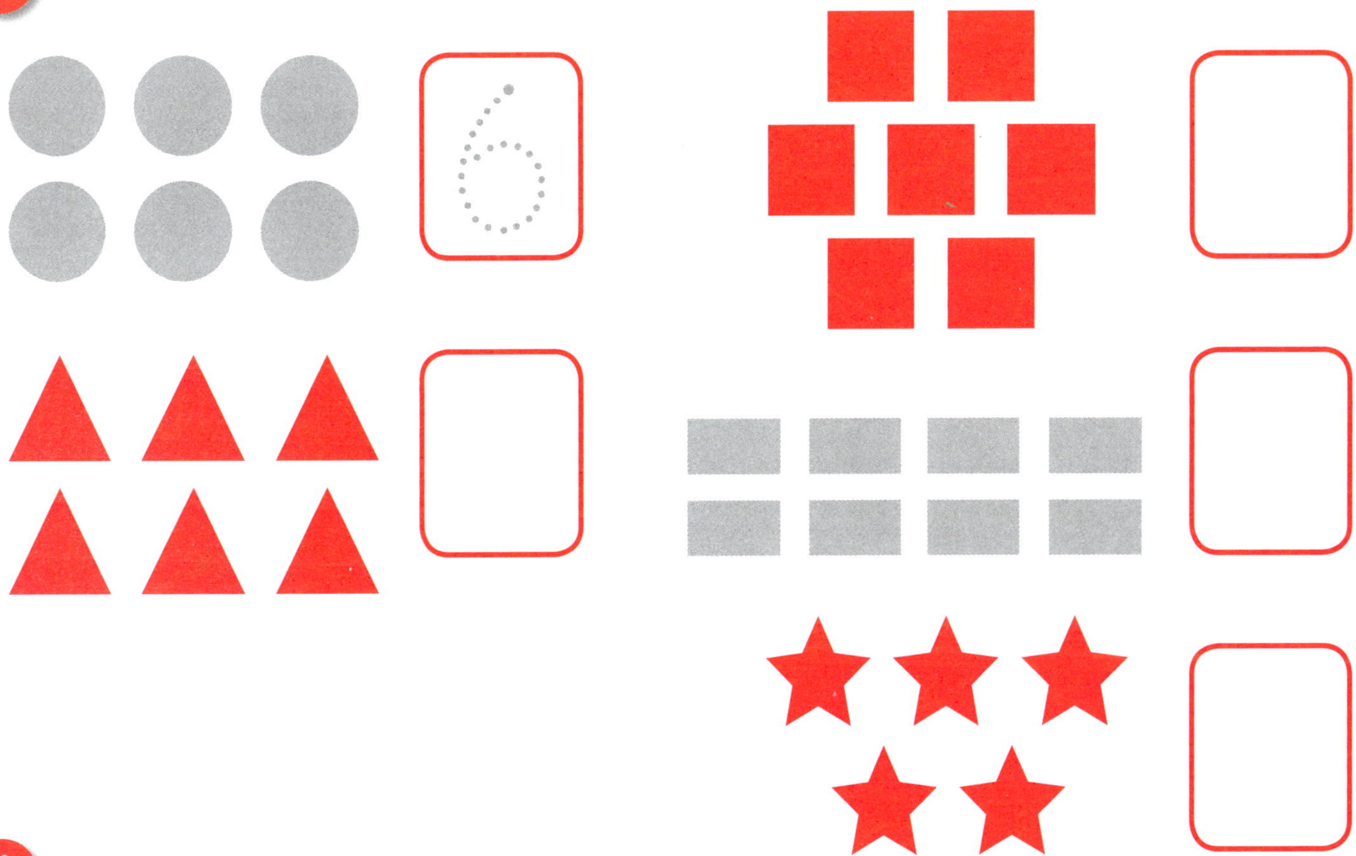

4 Draw.

3 Circle each group of shapes and count how many in each set. Write the total in the box.

4 Draw the next two shapes.

8 Lesson 3

1 Find, count and write.

2 Count and circle 8.

1 Find the animals and count them. Then write the total in the box.

2 Count and circle groups of 8.

3 Match and write.

$5 + 2 = \square$

$4 + 1 = 5$

$2 + 2 = \square$

$7 + 1 = \square$

$4 + 2 = \square$

3

Match the pictures and the sums.
Then complete the sums.

8 Lesson 4

1 Draw bees.

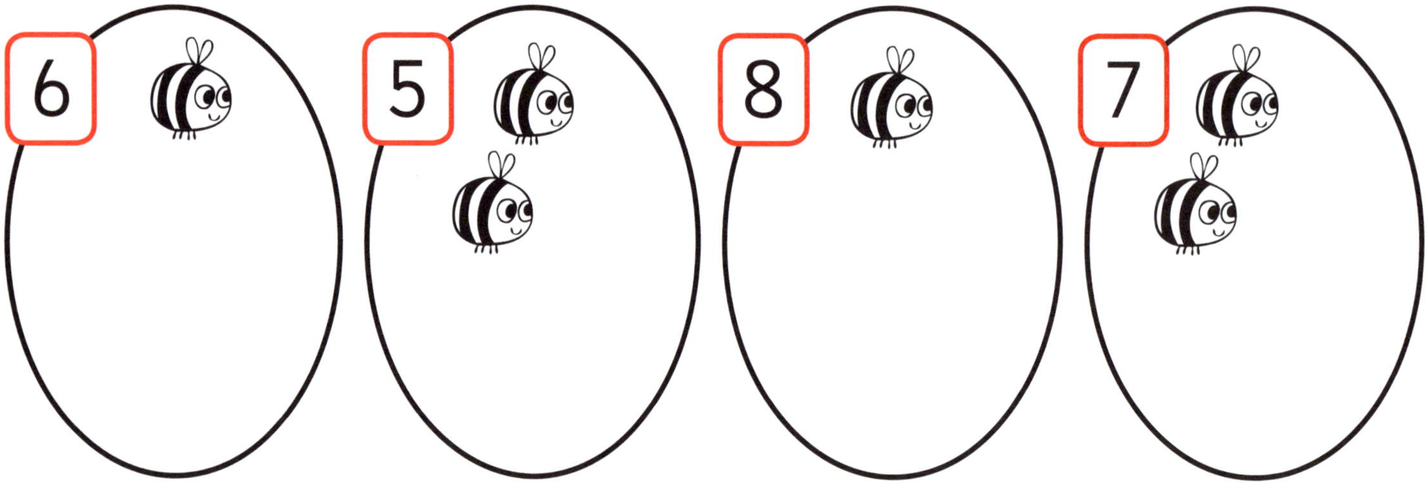

2 Draw.

3 Match.

six

five

seven

1 Draw bees to finish the sets.

2 Draw the next 2 pictures in the series.

3 Match the number word to the correct group.

4 Draw 1 more. Count and write.

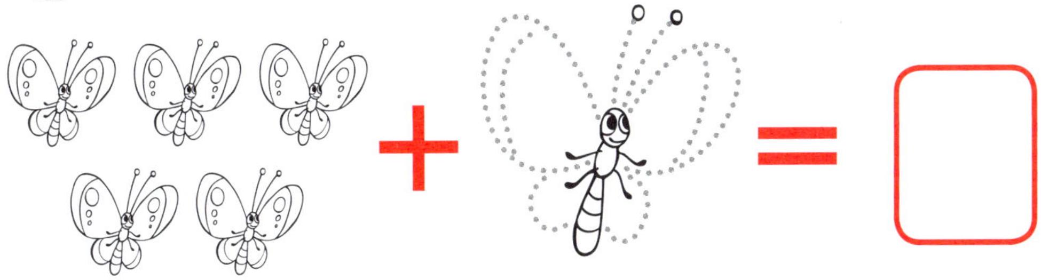

six 6

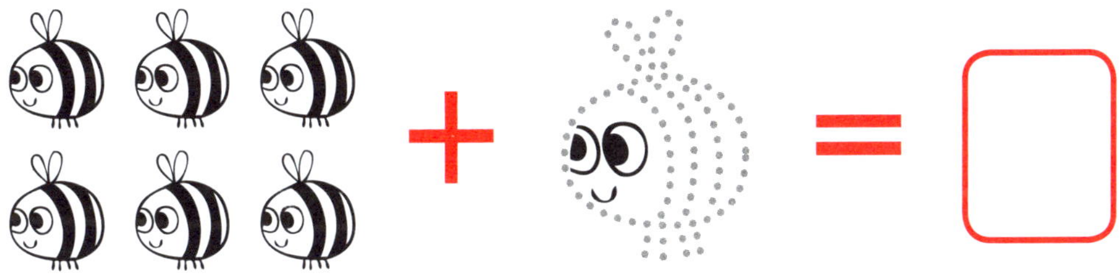

seven 7

eight 8

5 Trace. Find 8 and circle.

4

Draw one more. Then count and write the total in the box.

5

Trace numbers 1 to 8. Then find and circle 8 caterpillars hidden in the garden.

Unit 9 In the kitchen

Lesson 1

1 Count. Trace and write.

9 nine

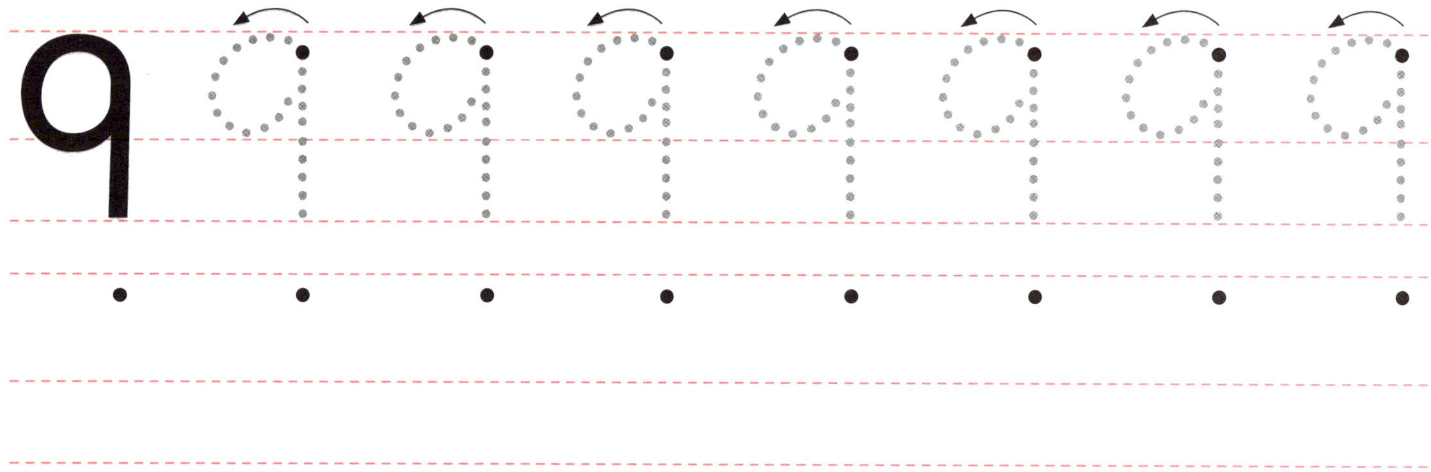

2 Count and write.

1 Count the cups. Trace and write number 9. Then write the number word nine.

2 Count the different items on the table and write the total in the box.

3 Count, write and match.

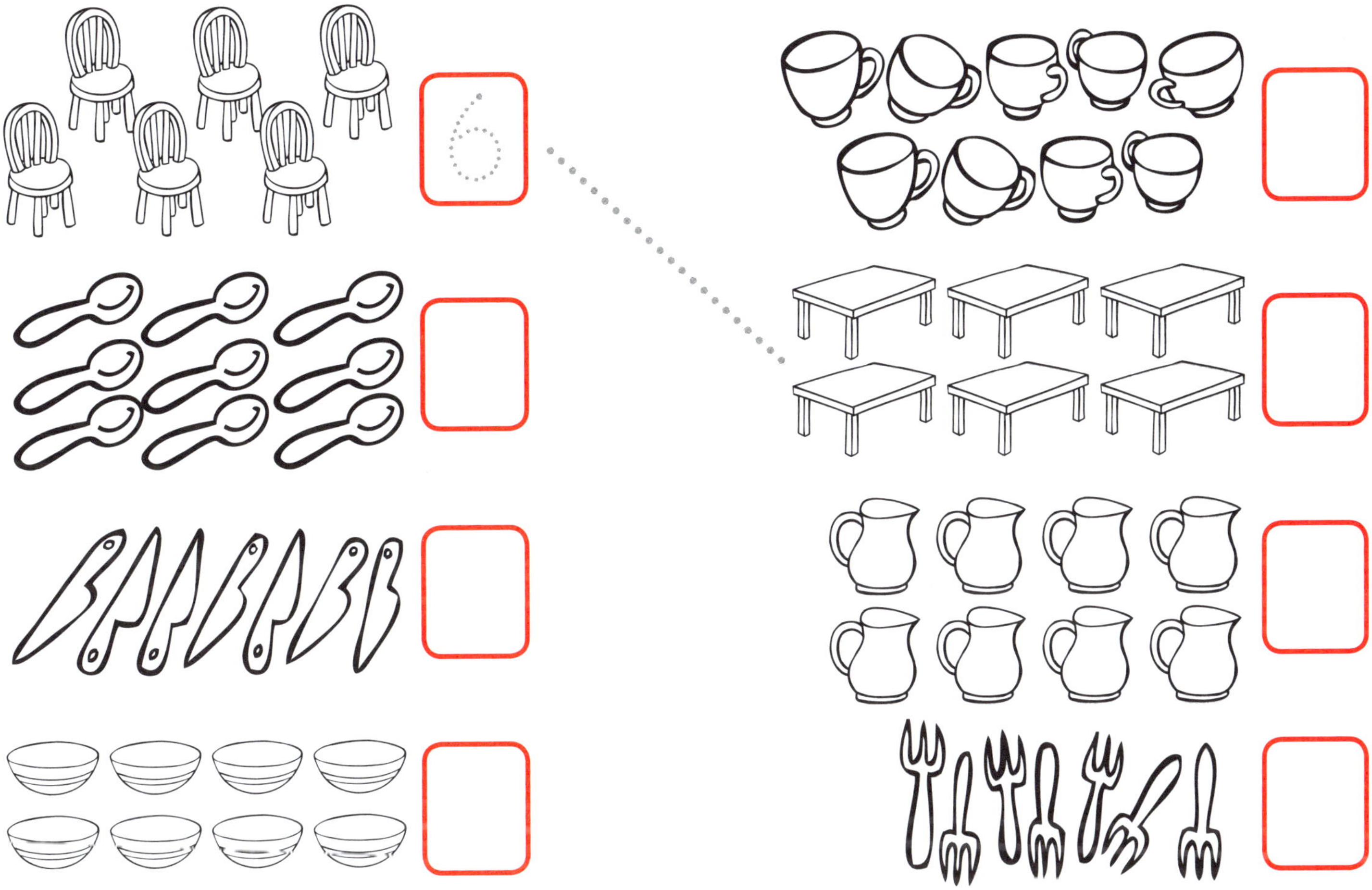

4 Draw.

3 Count the number of items and write the total in the box. Then match the groups with the same number.

4 Draw the next one.

9 Lesson 2

1 Find and circle.

1

Find the seven differences in the pictures.
Then circle the differences in the bottom picture.

2 Draw.

3 Choose a pattern. Draw.

1 Find, count and write.

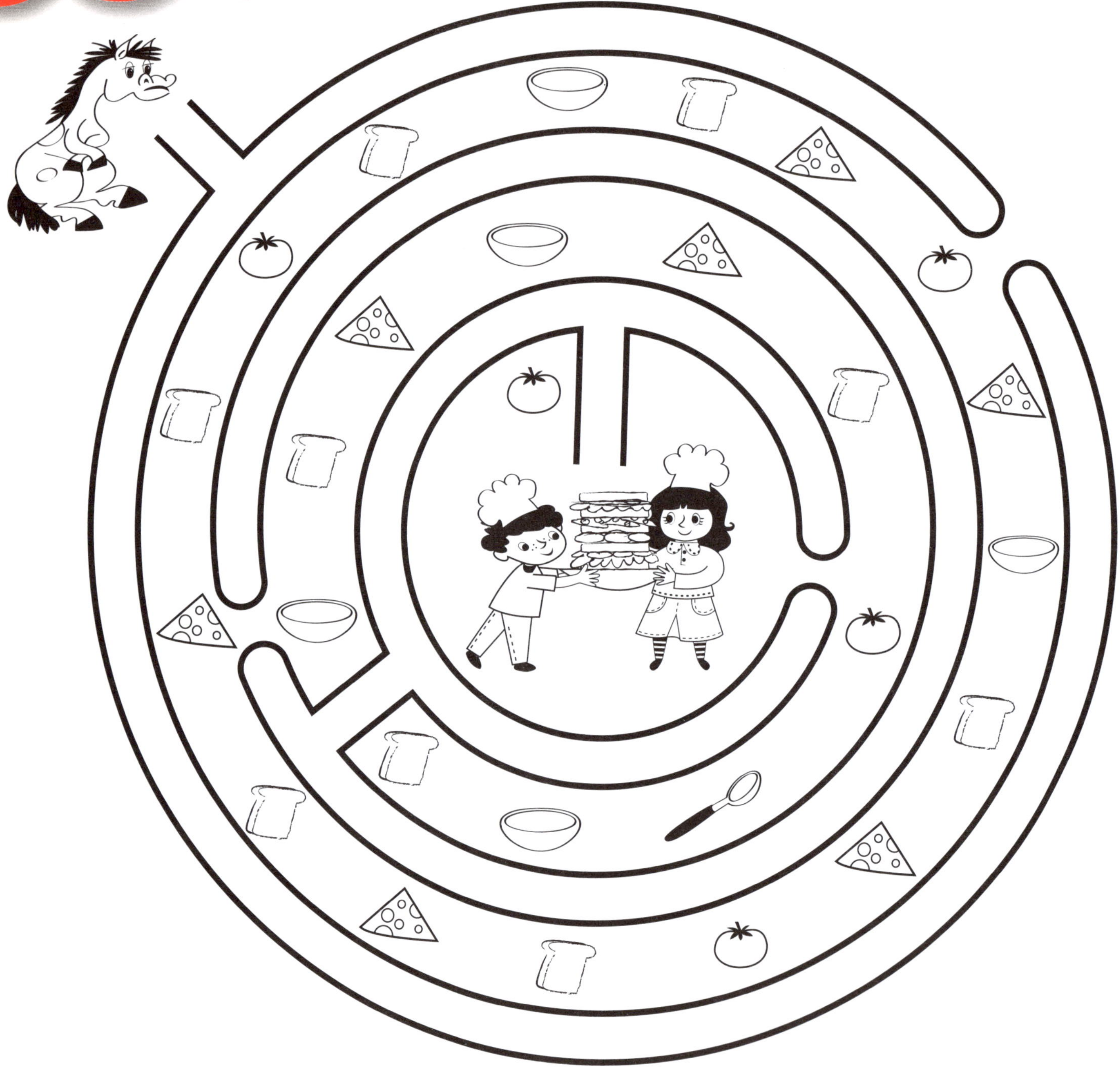

1

Trace through the maze and help Horsey find the sandwich. Then count the items and write the totals in the box.

2 Match.

in on under

3 Draw.

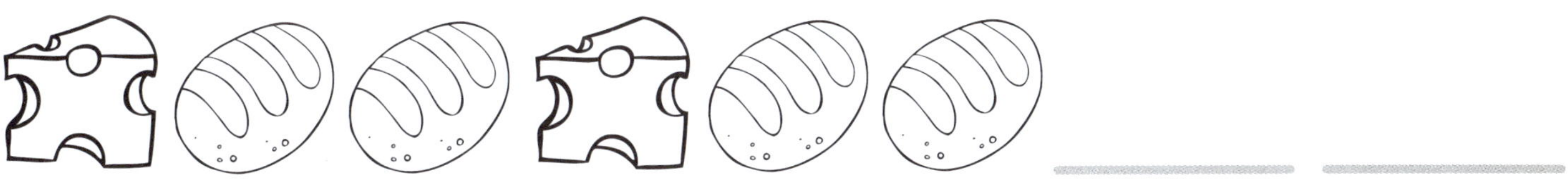

2 Match *in*, *on* and *under* to the correct pictures by drawing a line from the word on the top row to the picture below.

3 Draw the next two pictures.

9 Lesson 4

1 Count, write and circle.

2 3 4

3 4 5

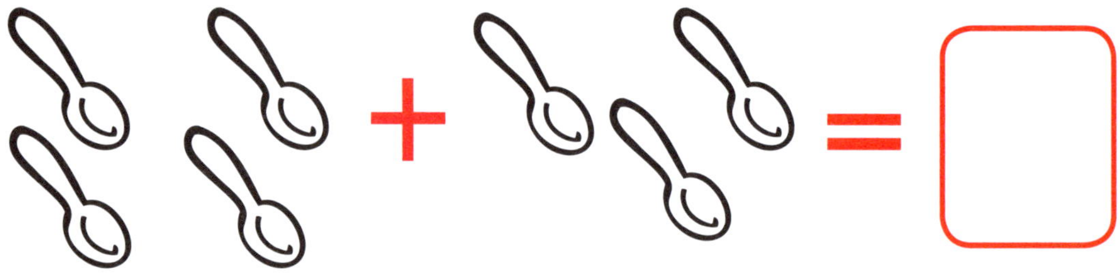

5 6 7

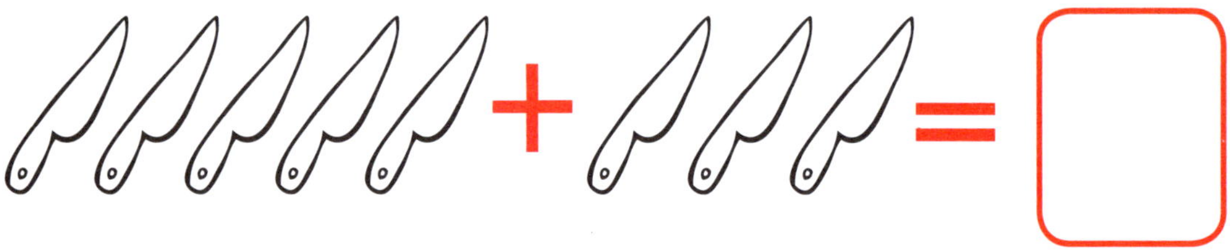

7 8 9

6 7 8

8 9 10

1

Count and write the totals in the boxes.
Then circle how many there are altogether.

2 Count and write.

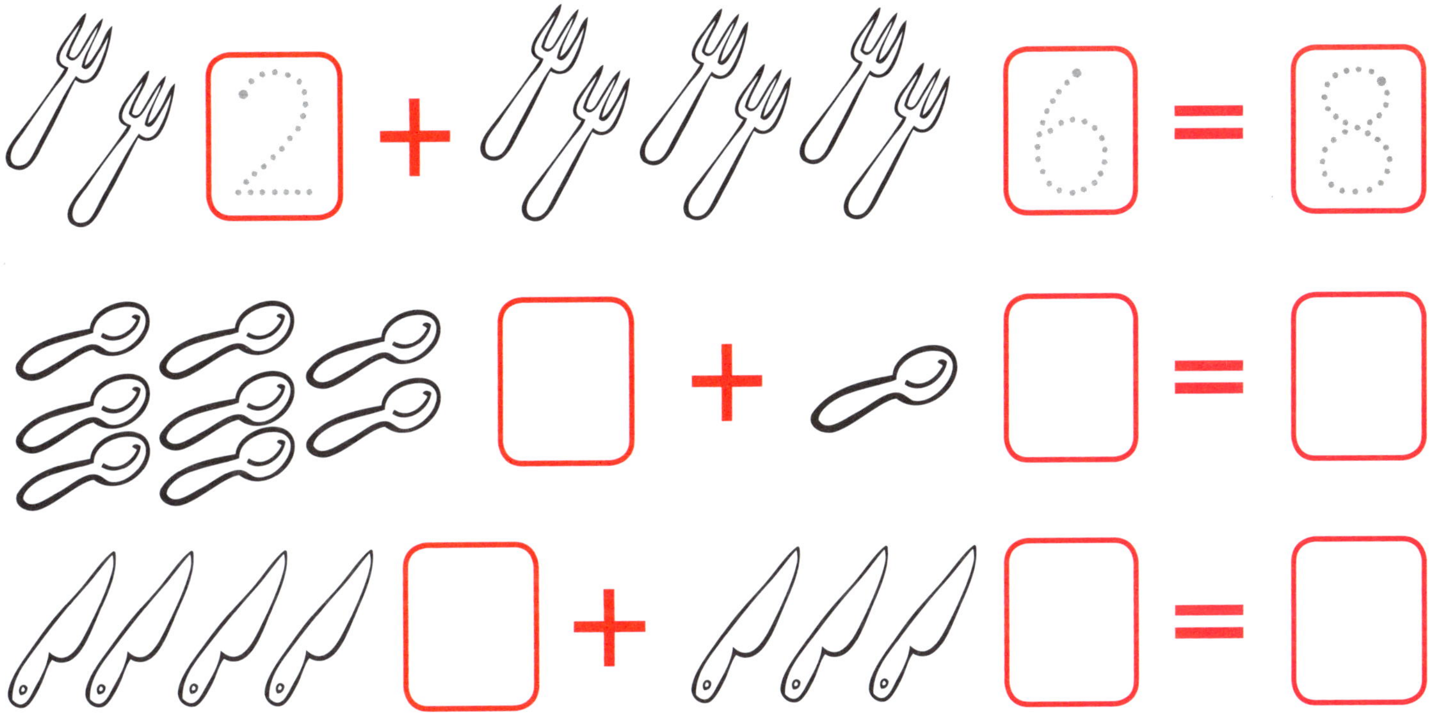

3 Trace. Find 9 and circle.

2 Count and write the numbers. Then add the numbers and write the total in the box.

3 Trace numbers 0-9. Then find and circle 9 bowls hidden in the garden.

Review 3

1 Match.

0 1 2 3 4 5 6 7 8 9

2 Count and write.

 4 +  3 = 7

 ☐ +  ☐ = ☐

 ☐ +  ☐ = ☐

1 Match the number on the top line to the correct number of buns on the plate below.

2 Count each group of animals and write the total in the box. Then add the numbers in the two groups and write the total.

3 Draw.

6

9

4 Match.

four six one nine five

1 2 3 4 5 6 7 8 9 10

eight two ten three seven

5 Write. 0 1 2 3 4 5 6 7 8 9 10

3 Draw the correct number of circles in each set.

4 Match the number word to the correct number.

5 Write the missing numbers on the caterpillar.

Unit 10 Lesson 1

Let's have a party!

1 Count. Trace and write.

10 ten

10 10 10 10 10 10

2 Draw. Count and write.

6 + ____ 2 = ☐

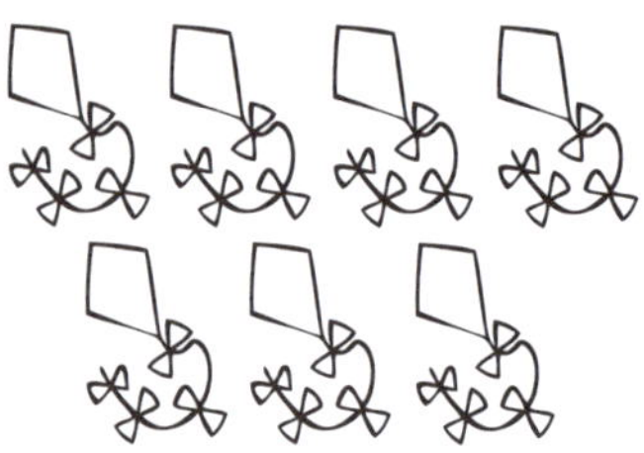

7 + ____ 2 = ☐

8 + ____ 2 = ☐

1 Count the ice-creams. Trace and write number 10 and the number word ten.

2 Draw 2 more. Then count and write the total in the box.

3 Find, count and write.

3

Find and count. Then write the numbers.

1 Draw. Count and write.

2 Count and write.

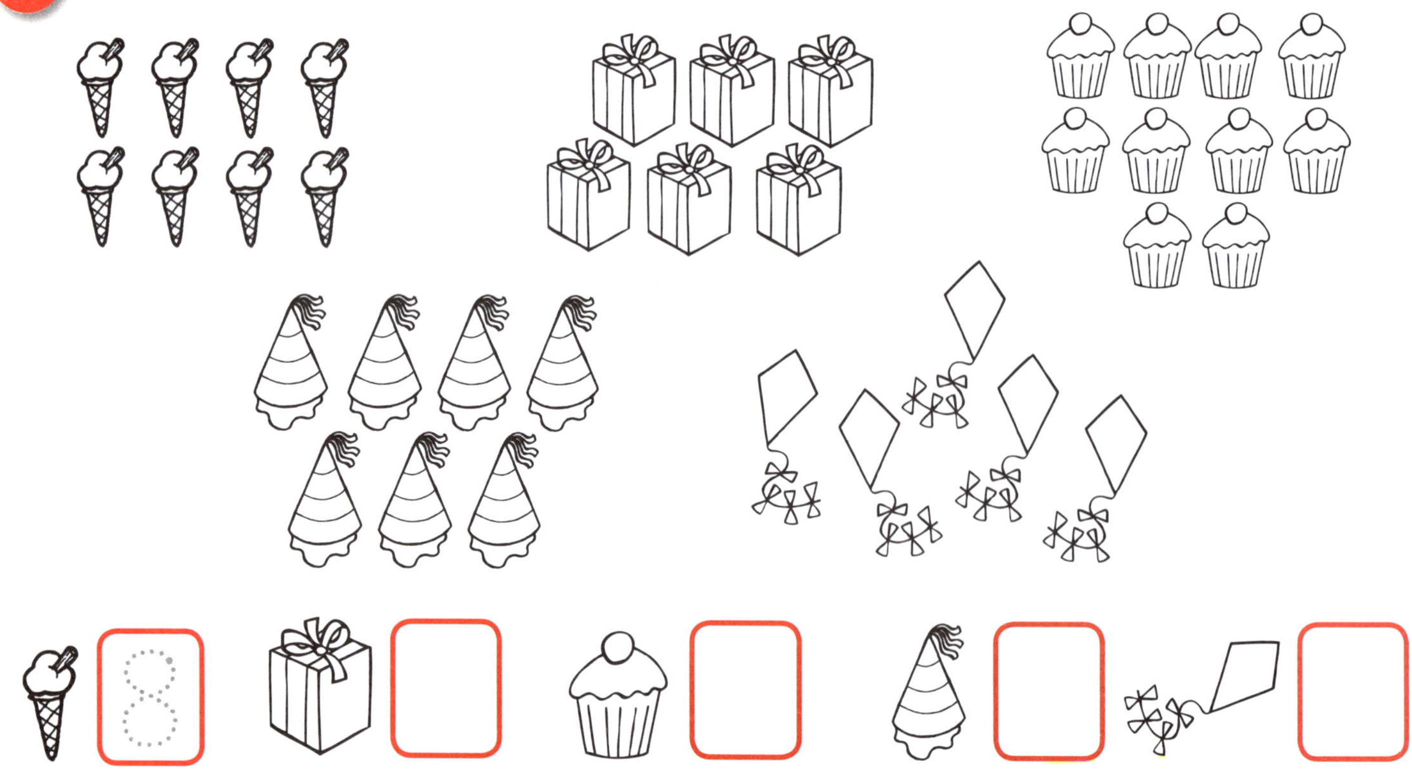

1 Draw an ice-cream for each child. Count and write the number 10 in the total box.

2 Count the number of items in each group and write the total in the box.

3 Match and draw.

6 six 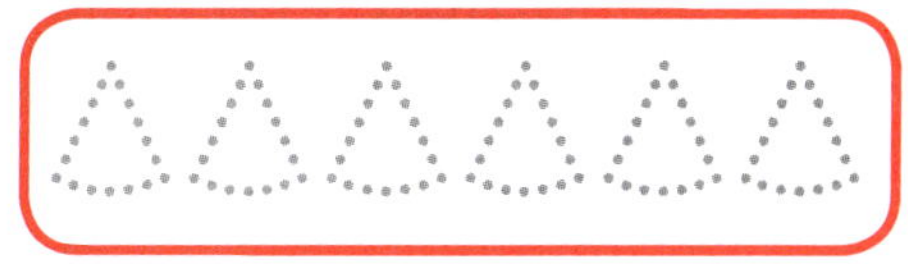

7 seven

8 eight

9 nine

4 Draw.

5 Write.

six 6

nine ____

seven ____

ten ____

eight ____

3 Match the numbers to the number word. Then draw the correct number of party hats.

4 Draw the correct number of presents in each set.

5 Read the number word and write the correct number.

10 Lesson 3

1 Colour.

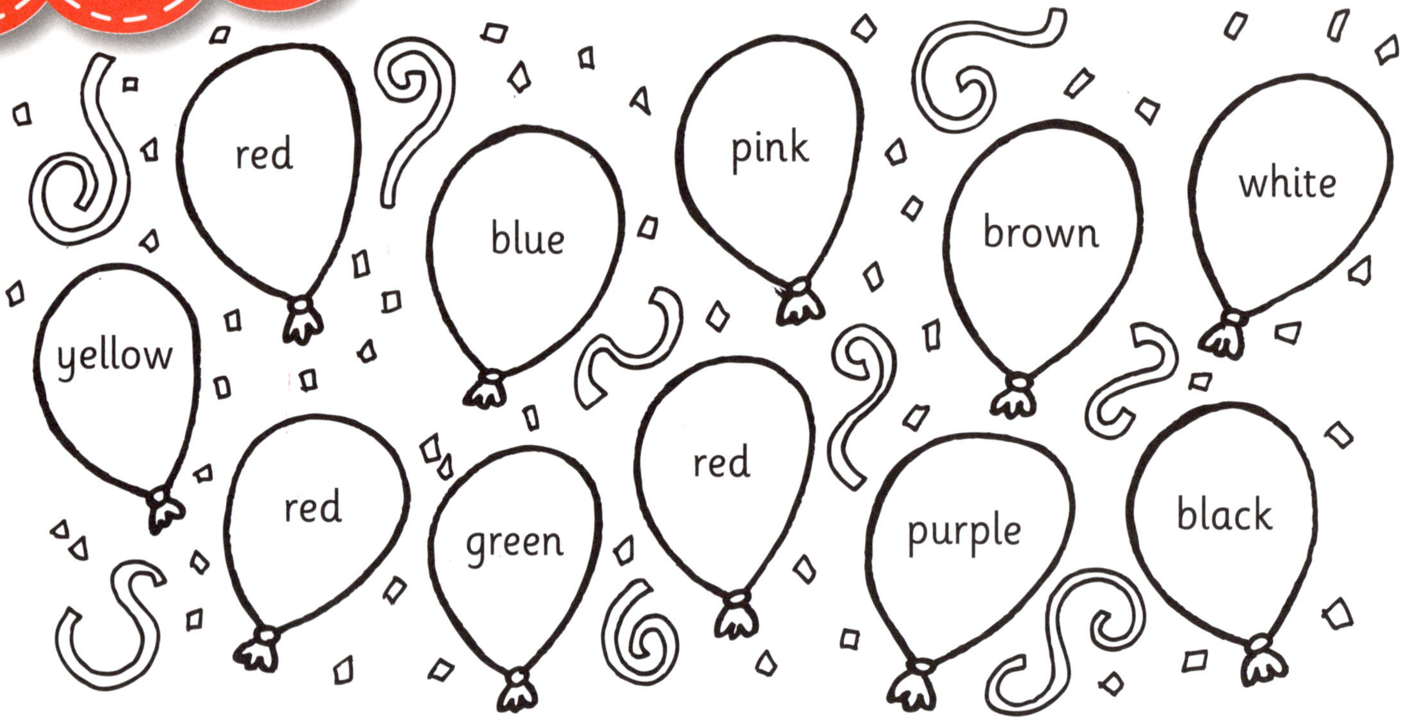

2 Count and match.

$1 + 2 = 3$

$3 + 2 = 5$

$6 + 1 = 7$

$4 + 3 = 7$

1 Colour the balloons according to the word on each.

2 Count and match the pictures to the correct sums.

3 Count and write.

1 2 3 4 5 6 7 8 9 10

4 Jump.

Jump 3

1 2 3 4 5 6 7 8 9 10 | 7

Jump 2

1 2 3 4 5 6 7 8 9 10 | ☐

Jump 1

1 2 3 4 5 6 7 8 9 10 | ☐

Jump 6

1 2 3 4 5 6 7 8 9 10 | ☐

Jump 4

1 2 3 4 5 6 7 8 9 10 | ☐

---

3 Count from 1 to 10 and write the numbers.

4 Jump with Bella. Write the number.

1 Write.

0 1 __ __ __ __ __ __ __ __ 10

2 Draw.

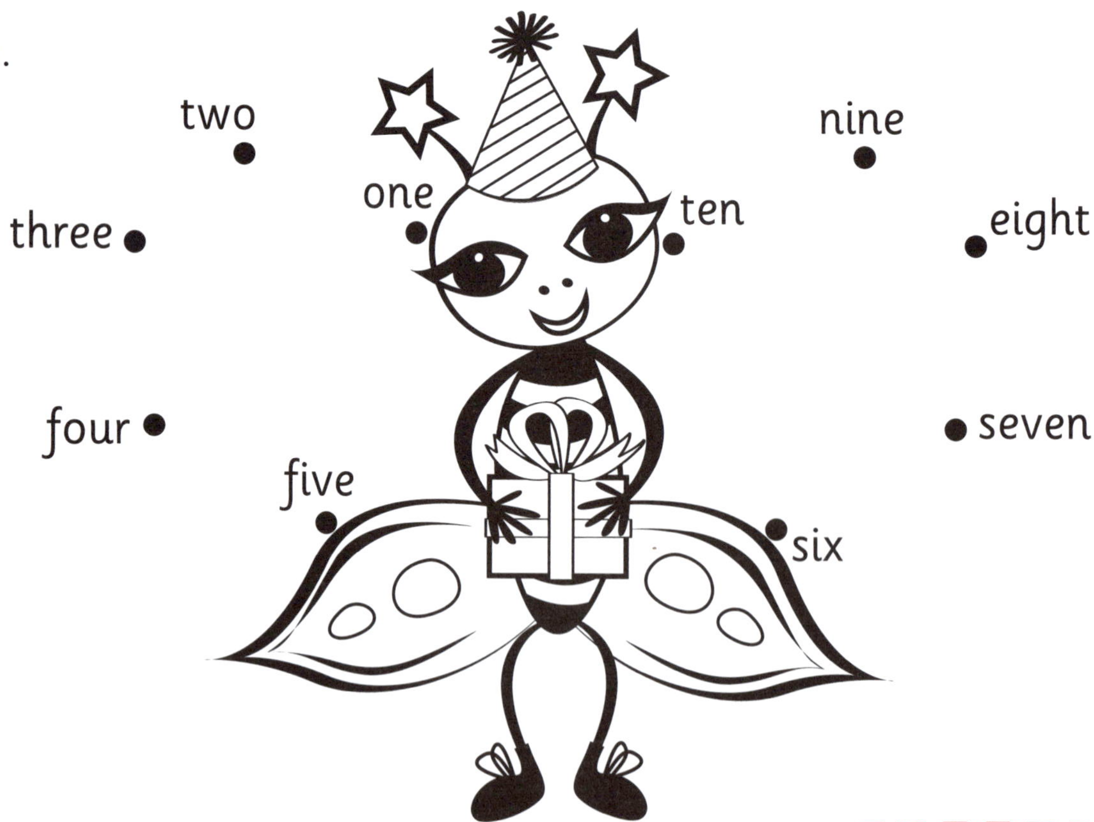

1 Look at the skateboards and write the numbers in order on the number line.

2 Join the dots from numbers 1 to 10.

3 Draw and write.

4 Match and trace.

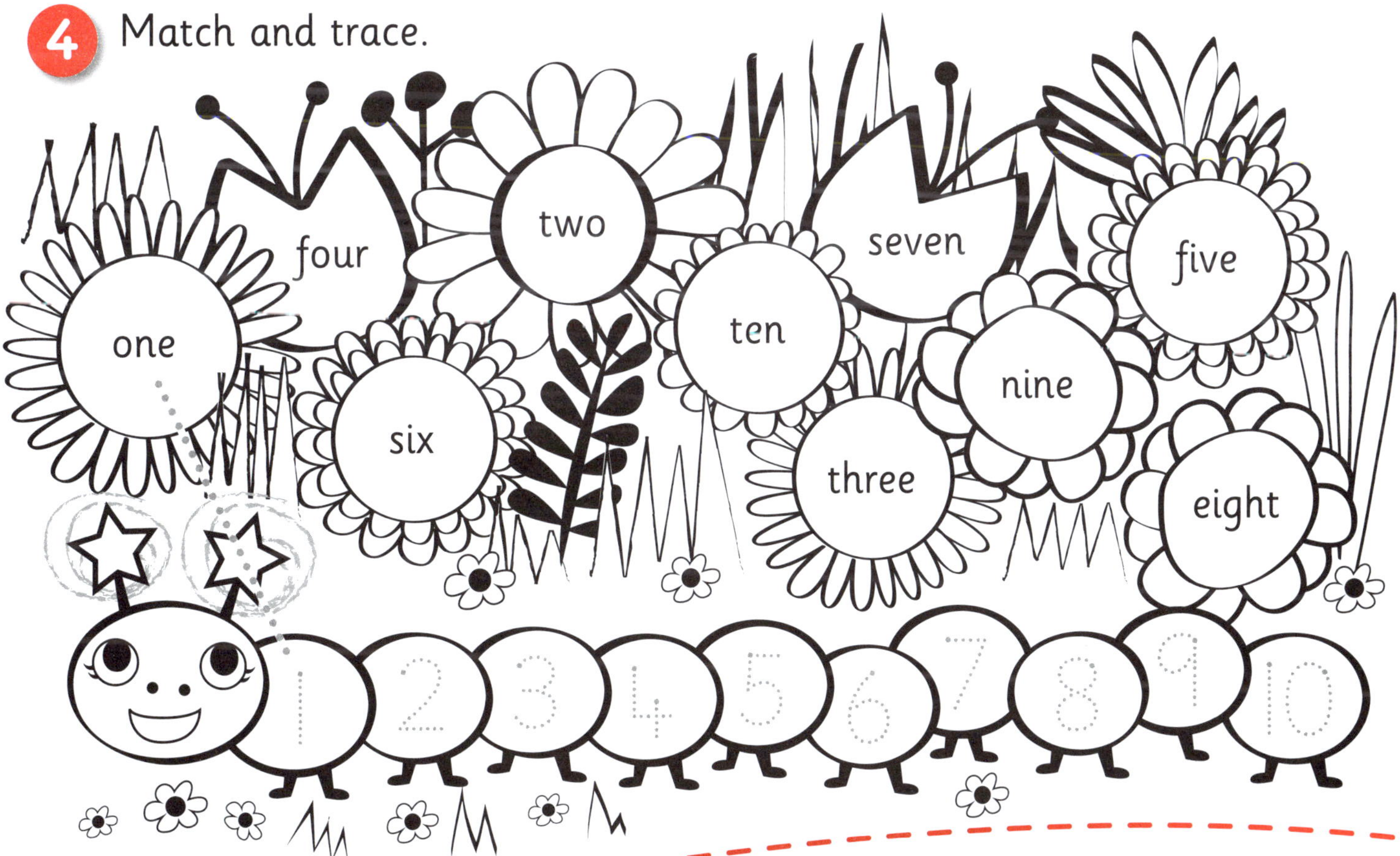

3 Draw 10 balloons and write numbers 1-10 in each.

4 Match the number words on the flowers to the numberline. Trace numbers 1-10.

Macmillan Education
4 Crinan Street
London N1 9XW
A division of Macmillan Publishers Limited

Companies and representatives throughout the world

ISBN 978-0-230-45567-2

Written by Jill Leighton

First published 2014

Designed by Liz Adcock
Illustrated by Liz Adcock, Simon Smith, Joseph Wilkins
Cover design concept by Astwood Design Consultancy
Cover illustration by Liz Adcock

Author's acknowledgement
I would like to thank my Editor and team for making the project such a fulfilling experience and also for their professionalism and inspiration.

Printed and bound in India

2018

10 9 8 7 6